Bush Ballads and Galloping Rhymes
EDITED & ILLUSTRATED

Adam Lindsay Gordon

Edited & introduced by Denis Daly
Biographical sketch by Douglas Sladen
Preface by Marcus Clarke

Voices of Today
Australia

Copyright © Voices of Today
Willetton, Western Australia.

All rights reserved. No part of this book may be reproduced in any form without written permission from the publisher, excepting those parts of the text already in the public domain.

Cover image: "The Sick Stockrider" by Charlie Hammond, 1905.
State Library of Victoria, ID1679478, out of copyright.
Cover design by Voices of Today © 2022

BUSH BALLADS & GALLOPING RHYMES

Adam Lindsay Gordon

Edited & introduced by Denis Daly
Biographical sketch by Douglas Sladen
Preface by Marcus Clarke

CONTENTS

Publisher's Note	7
Introduction	2
Adam Lindsay Gordon: A Biographical Sketch	8
Preface	30
A Dedication	37
The Sick Stockrider	42
The Swimmer	47
From the Wreck	51
No Name	57
Wolf and Hound	61
De Te	65
How We Beat the Favourite	69
Fragmentary Scenes from the Road to Avernus	75
Doubtful Dreams	92
The Rhyme of Joyous Garde	98
Thora's Song	110
The Three Friends	112
A Song of Autumn	118
The Romance of Britomarte	119
Laudamus	132
A Basket of Flowers	134
A Fragment	138
Review: The Argus (Melbourne)	141

Publisher's Note

This volume includes faithful reproductions of historical texts. As such, certain attitudes and expressions that are today recognised as inappropriate or problematic may be present in the text. These are retained to faithfully represent the historical attitudes of the original authors, but do not represent the attitudes or values of the publisher. The texts should be interpreted with critical awareness. Some obvious typographical errors have been corrected, and minor editorial insertions have been made for clarity.

Monument to Adam Lindsay Gordon at Mount Gambier
Photograph ca.1900
State Library of South Australia, B-48399.

Introduction

By Denis Daly

The classic Australian poets who are most famous today are those who were born and grew up in Australia. The works of poets like Henry Lawson and Andrew Barton "Banjo" Paterson are set in a post-colonial world in which Australia had progressed from being a collection of penal settlements, to being an independent nation.

However, the forbears who influenced these poets were immigrants, many of whom were attracted to the new land by the promise of prosperity from mining exploration (for gold in particular) and through pastoral enterprises. Among the adventurous souls who made Australia their new home were the poets J. Lionel Michael, Robert Sealy, R. H. Horne, Henry Kingsley and Adam Lindsay Gordon.

With the development of major population centres came the establishment of newspapers and periodicals, which gave scope to the publication of new literature. *The Argus* (Melbourne) newspaper first appeared in 1846 and *The Australasian*, established in 1854, quickly became the most important literary journal in Australia. Papers, even those devoted to sports, were very willing to accept contributions in verse and represented the first opportunity for many poets to be published in print.

Adam Lindsay Gordon was born in Charlton Kings near Cheltenham, UK, in 1833. He landed in Adelaide in 1853 and immediately obtained a position in the mounted police. Two years later, he resigned from this position and took up a job as a horse breaker, an occupation which led him into horse racing. Horses and horse riding are subjects that occur frequently in Gordon's verse.

In 1864, he published a little book of verse at Mt. Gambier, South Australia, and began to contribute verses to a Melbourne sporting paper in 1866. These were printed anonymously and attracted some attention; but a collection of his ballads, "Sea Spray and Smoke Drift," published in 1867, attracted little praise and generated negligible profit.

After a series of crushing disappointments, Gordon committed suicide in Melbourne on 24th June, 1870. His second collection of poetry, "Bush Ballads and Galloping Rhymes," was published the day after his death.

The dramatic conclusion to Gordon's life awakened public sympathy and stimulated interest in his writings. It was soon found that in both the city and the bush, many of his spirited racing ballads were well known. The virile, athletic tone of his verse, which taught:

> How a man should uphold the sports of his land
> And strike his best with a strong right hand
> And take his strokes in return—

and his practical philosophy, summed up in the well-known quatrain—

> Life is mostly froth and bubble,

> Two things stand like stone;
> Kindness in another's trouble,
> Courage in your own—

appealed to many Australians. Gordon's work cannot be considered as peculiarly Australian in character; but much of it is concerned with horses, and all of it throbs with the manly, reckless personality of the writer. Horses and horse-racing are a prominent part of Australian culture; even people who were not conversant with literature found that the Swinburnian rush of Gordon's ballads charmed their ears.

In his lifetime Gordon enjoyed the support of some influential admirers, notably Marcus Clarke, fellow poet Henry Kendall, and critic and anthologist Douglas Sladen. Due to their efforts, his reputation did not fade after his untimely death. His verse also attracted attention in England, and later become the subject of mockery by George Bernard Shaw in his last play, *Shakes versus Shav*.

In the 1880s, Gordon's works were widely disseminated and recital of his verse became a pastime of rural workers across Australia. Gordon may be considered the first really popular poet in Australian literary history, paving the way for later, and more celebrated poets, such as A. B. "Banjo" Paterson, C.J. Dennis and Henry Lawson.

Gordon was one of the first Australian poets for whom memorials have been created. Dingley Dell, located near Mount Gambier, South Australia, was the poet's home between 1864 and 1865, and has since been converted into a museum. In 1932, a statue to Gordon's memory was unveiled near Parliament House, Melbourne, and in 1934, a bust of Gordon was unveiled in Westminster Abbey, London, by the Duke of York.

Included in this special edition of "Bush Ballads and Galloping Rhymes" are the eighteen poems included in the original publication, an essay on Gordon by Douglas Sladen, a preface by Marcus Clarke, and a review of the book that appeared in the Melbourne newspaper, *The Argus*, on 28th June, 1870.

SOURCES:

Howlett-Ross, J. *A Memoir of the Life of Adam Lindsay Gordon*. London: W. W. Gibbings, 1892.

Turner, Henry Gyles and Alexander Sutherland. *The Development of Australian Literature*. London: Longmans, Green, and Co., 1898.

Gordon, Adam Lindsay and Douglas Sladen, ed. *The Poems of Adam Lindsay Gordon*. New York: G. P. Putnam's Sons, 1913.

Adam Lindsay Gordon. *The Poems of Adam Lindsay Gordon* (with preface by Marcus Clarke). London: Ward, Lock & Co., n.d.

Stevens, Bertram, ed. *An Anthology of Australian Verse*. Sydney: Angus & Robertson, 1906.

Adam Lindsay Gordon

Adam Lindsay Gordon: A Biographical Sketch

By Douglas Sladen

A brief account of Gordon's short life will conduce to the better understanding of his poems.

He was the direct descendant of the original Adam of Gordon, who was rewarded with the Gordon country in Aberdeenshire for deserting from Edward I. to the Bruce; of the Gordon who was killed in the great battle of Pinkie; of the Marquess of Huntly, who laid down his head as finely as Montrose for his king; of the Gordon who was out in the Forty-five; of the Peterborough of the Spanish Succession; of a Duke of Gordon and an Earl of Aberdeen. And his mother was brought up by the brother of the Lady Anne Lindsay who wrote 'Auld Robin Gray.' His father, Captain Adam Durnford Gordon, was a dashing Indian officer who settled successively in the Azores, the Madeiras, and at Cheltenham. Adam Lindsay was born in the Azores on October 19, 1833. He was sent to Cheltenham College at the immature age of seven, on the day that it opened its doors, and there he was received by the future Lord James of Hereford, who showed signs of a remarkable future by arriving at the school a day before the time.

After he had been at school a year, Lindsay disappears from the College register and the ken of every biographer for six years, when he appears as a cadet of the

Royal Military Academy at Woolwich, where he was the contemporary and intimate friend of Gordon of Khartoum and 'Gunner Jingo.' Perhaps he was abroad part of the time, for he told Tenison Woods that he had been in France, and he was fond of reciting French poetry. He was at Woolwich three years, and left it, whether by request or by his own free will, without obtaining a commission. Even there he was famous for his escapades. There is a general consensus that he was a dashing and high-spirited boy. That dash, those high spirits, were destined to get him into trouble. For about the time that he went to Woolwich, he took to spending his holidays in Jem Edwards the prize-fighter's boxing saloon at the Roebuck Inn, Cheltenham, and in Tom Oliver's training stables out at Prestbury, where he met some of the most famous sporting personages of the day. This bore an unexpected fruit when, at the conclusion of his Woolwich career, he was sent to the Royal Grammar School at Worcester. For there he distinguished himself by stealing a mare from her stable to ride her in the steeplechase. This mare was the often-quoted Lallah Rookh, and the attendant scandal is believed to have been one of the causes which sent Gordon out to Australia. He was at the Worcester Grammar School for a year or more, and then went back to Cheltenham College for a year. How a boy with a past, eighteen years old, came to be readmitted there has not been explained.

A year later, after (as we learn from her own letters) offering to forfeit his passage if the beautiful Jane Bridges would marry him, he sailed for Australia and began the serious part of his life. Hitherto, as his letters to Charley

Walker show, he had varied the monotony of a strict Low Church home with skylarking and debts.[1] If his father, the Cheltenham Colonel Newcome, was disposed to be lenient, his mother, very proud of their lineage, was not – so it gradually became imperative that he should go. In Cheltenham he might have been a mere hanger-on of sport. In Australia, where he landed in November 1853, his character developed from the first. Enlisting at once in the South Australian Police as a constable (though his father had obtained a commission for him), he found himself in a disciplined but exciting life, and for the first time regularly occupied with horses, though he had owned a horse and won a couple of steeplechases in England.

We find him breaking in and training, owning and riding a steeplechaser before he had been in Australia a year, and two years after his landing, resigning from the police to be a wandering horse-breaker, an avocation which he followed with the utmost zest for seven years.

It was in these years, riding from station to station, that he acquired the knowledge of the bush and bushmen displayed in his poems, and the intuition into the characters of horses which gave him such a wonderful command over his mount in a race. When his work was done he saw little of the stockmen and their master. Unless he was invited to stay in the squatter's house, he pitched his tent a mile away, and spent his evenings in reading

---

[1] Charley Walker, son of the famous gentleman-rider of the same name, was a Worcester friend of Gordon's own age, who married a sister of Jane Bridges. Fourteen most characteristic letters written by Gordon to him, some in England, some in Australia, are given in *Adam Lindsay Gordon and his friend in England and Australia*.

Gordon's Leap, Mt Gambier road.
Sketch by Charlie Hammond, ca.1910–1920
State Library of Victoria, ID1678508.

and, as time went on, in writing by the feeble light of a sludge lamp. Tenison Woods, the Roman Catholic priest of a district of 22,000 square miles, who met him by chance at Lake Hawdon station, whose owner, Mr. Stockdale, made a friend of him, had a long talk with him about books, and placed his library at his disposal. The book Gordon loved best was a *Horace* to carry about in his lonely rides.

In 1862 he married Maggie Park, who had nursed him after a bad fall at the Caledonian Hotel at Robe, South Australia. In 1864 he received a legacy of £7000 (after two years' search by the trustees to discover his where-abouts). He bought a few small properties, and was persuaded to stand for Parliament. An attempt was being made by the Blyth Government to break up the squatters' properties, and a candidate was needed who sympathised with them, and himself commanded the sympathies of the lower classes. Gordon, as the most daring horse-breaker in the colony, and the beau-ideal of the bushman in his code of honour and manliness, was the best possible candidate, and was returned at the head of the poll.

In the South Australian Parliament, though his ideas about land legislation were good, and have since become law, Gordon was a failure. The slowness of the proceedings wearied him. His own speeches, stuffed with classical allusions, were ill-delivered and over the hoods of his audience. All he got out of Parliament lay in his long hours of hard study in the magnificent library. His properties began to turn out badly, he lost money on the racecourse, and in less than two years threw up his seat.

Right at the beginning of his parliamentary career he made himself famous by winning the principal steeplechase at the Adelaide Races. He had already won many local steeplechases and was soon to win important steeplechases in Victoria, famous all over the world for its steeplechasing.

From this time forward, events hurried him on to 'Glory coupled with an early tomb.'

He sold his cottage in Adelaide, and determined to live in his old home in the Mount Gambier district of South Australia, on the wreck of his fortune, and what he could make out of writing. He had already, in 1865 and 1860, contributed 'Ye Wearie Wayfarer' and 'Hippodromania' to the Melbourne papers.

In September 1867, Gordon had released his first volumes, *Sea-Spray and Smoke-Drift* and *Ashtaroth*. Also in 1867, he started a livery business in Ballarat, taking the stables of the principal hotel, where he was soon joined by Harry Mount, brother of Lambton Mount, his partner on his West Australian station. This, partly owing to a bad accident, partly to his unbusinesslike habits, resulted in a disastrous failure within a year, and finally, after paying visits in Melbourne for several months, he settled there in the middle of 1869 to make a living as he could.

On October 5th, 1868, he seems to have left Ballarat for good, and to have come to Melbourne on a visit to Robert Power, the first of a series of visits which lasted till the middle of 1869. Almost immediately he began a remarkable list of successes. At a bound he became the most famous steeplechase rider in Australia.

On October 10th, 1869, he won three steeplechases in one day at the Melbourne Steeplechase meeting, on

Babbler, Viking, and Cadger; and a month later he won the V.R.C. steeplechase on Viking. His best poems almost synchronised, for he wrote 'A Song of Autumn ' in October or November 1868, and published 'Doubtful Dreams' in *The Colonial Monthly* of December 1868, while in January 1869 he wrote, reclining on a bough of an old gum-tree at Yallum, 'The Sick Stockrider,' 'How We Beat the Favourite,' 'From the Wreck,' and 'Wolf and Hound.'

He went on winning steeplechases to the middle of 1869, and writing fine poems at intervals. Then he established himself and his wife in the lodging at Brighton, which proved to be his last home. From that time onwards he seems to have won few races and written few poems. In truth, his mind was beginning to be filled up with the idea of succeeding to the Esslemont estate, to which, as head of his family, his friends at home believed him to be entitled.

Esslemont is a fine mansion in Aberdeenshire, with a good rent-roll attached to it, and, though Gordon had no desire to play the laird, he would have liked the income to help him to provide for his wife; and he doubtless would have liked those who had refused to allow him to compete in the Ladies' Purse Steeplechase in South Australia to see him installed in the 'Barony' of Esslemont. The sporting chance he had of obtaining it did not conduce to his following up quietly the fair prospects and the fame of a career of steeplechasing, training, and writing which lay open before him, and in March 1870 the need of immediate ready money made him accept, against his judgment, the mount on Prince Rupert which led to the fall from which he never properly recovered. When, three months later, he had the further misfortune to have his hopes of Esslemont dashed to the ground, while at the same time his monetary troubles were closing round him, he just waited to see his last and best volume, *Bush Ballads and Galloping Rhymes*, through the press, and went out and shot himself the first thing on the following morning,

    A whole chapter of accidents prevented any interference with his mad purpose. His friend Mr. Prendergast, whom he tried to see on his way to the scene of the suicide, was out. The Riddochs, his best friends in the hour of need, were far away in South Australia, and, when he actually lay dead in the scrub, were planning to make him come and stay with them lest he should do violence to himself after the bad news about Esslemont. And, worst of all, Lambton Mount, his chivalrous and much-loved partner in Western Australia, who could have stopped it by raising his little finger, arrived in Melbourne a week after his death, having wasted more than that time in looking for a lost horse. Mr. Mount told me this with his own lips, and mentioned at the same time the terrible loss which English literature has suffered by his carrying out the instructions in the last letter Gordon ever wrote to him: 'Please burn that old trunk of mine. Give the shepherds my old clothes; take the trunk and put it on the fire – turn it upside down on the campfire without looking at or reading anything.' If Lambton Mount had known that Gordon had contemplated suicide, not one of the many quires of manuscript written on lined blue foolscap (the paper on which Gordon always wrote) would have been destroyed. As it was, only one escaped. 'About a week afterwards,' added Mr Mount, 'one of the shepherds came back to me – he couldn't read. "I found this paper," he said, "in the pocket of the breeches, sir, which you gave me that belonged to Mr. Gordon." It was the poem which begins, "All night I've heard the marsh frog's croak." I sent it to *The Australasian*.'

And Mr. Mount told me that the loss was aggravated by the fact that Mrs. Gordon also burnt a box of Gordon's manuscripts after his death, to avoid the expense of removal.

Gordon and he lived together for six whole months on end, seeing each other all day and every day, and he was left with a passionate admiration for Gordon.

Gordon, he says, was the finest man he ever met in the course of his adventurous career. He was the sort of man who always took the heavy end of the log. There was only one thing that could make him depart a hair's breadth from the truth, and that was to save a man's life or a woman's honour. He never demanded a receipt. To give examples of Gordon's courage, physical and moral, would be unending repetition. Mr. Mount records a hitherto unrecorded accident which Gordon had about six months before his death, which would account for his unwillingness to ride Prince Rupert. Gordon was staying with Mr. Mount's brother Harry at a farm outside Ballarat. He was riding a colt 'that could jump a house,' and put him at a five-rail fence. 'Stop, Gordon!' cried Harry

Mount, 'the ground is rotten!' But Gordon put him at it, and the horse struck the top rail. Being a good rider he was not shot over the fence, where the ground was soft and he would have been clear of the horse, but kept his seat, and the horse rolled on him, crushing one complete side and his head. Blood came out of his eyes, nose, ears, and mouth. He did not recover consciousness for four days. Harry Mount went back, got his buggy, and drove him into Ballarat Hospital. His mind was never quite right afterwards.

Lambton Mount says that the poem called 'The Old Leaven,' which Gordon only wrote in the rough and never finished, was autobiographical. It was written on the night before he left Gordon to go to Western Australia. They were at the theatre together, hearing quite a good Italian opera company. Before the opera was over, Gordon went out, and Mr. Mount, when he got to the hotel, found him writing a poem at high steam. When Mr. Mount went in, Gordon went on writing without looking up, repeating out loud the lines:

> Who knows! Not I; I can hardly vouch
> For the truth of what little I see;
> And, now, if you've any weed in your pouch,
> Just hand it over to me.

Mr. Mount, not understanding, handed him his pouch, and Gordon wrote no more.

The latest information which has reached me from Australia itself is the very important article contributed to the *Sydney Mail* by Mr. W. Farmer Whyte, drawn from the Gordon manuscripts which he has lately purchased from Mrs. Kelly, who was Gordon's landlady at Brighton, near Melbourne, at the time of his death. There were two paragraphs in it relating to facts hitherto unknown to me, the correspondence of Gordon's uncle, Captain R.C.H. Gordon, with Mr. Kelly, and a love affair which Gordon had in Australia before he met his wife.

'Among the papers there is also a bill for rent, which reads as follows:

A. L. Gordon
Dr. to W.H. Kelly.
37 weeks' rent at £1 per week: £37 0 0
Eggs: £ 3 15 8
Total: £40 15 8

'Apparently after Gordon's death Mr. Kelly had written to the poet's uncle in England in reference to this debt, for I find the following letter, signed R.C.H. Gordon, and dated August 31, 1871:

'My Dear Mr. Kelly,
 I received your letter dated 16th June '71.
 It gave me great pleasure to hear from you, and to know how very kind you had been to my nephew, Lindsay Gordon, as Major Baker had told me. I will give him your thanks if I had an opportunity.
 No cause was assigned to me for my nephew's last act. I suppose he was troubled about money; and I know of

the strangeness of manner in the family. I have heard no more of Mrs. Lindsay Gordon than that Mr. Robt. Power sent her my little help. I am very sorry I cannot repay you more. I fear £30 is still due to you.

Lindsay's poems are very much by all my friends to whom I have lent them, as truly poetical and clever. I am very much obliged to you for your nice letter.

I remain yours truly obliged for your kindness to L. Gordon,
R.C.H. Gordon.'

Among the many tributes to the poet are four short lines which remind me that Gordon had loved and been loved before he met Maggie Park. They are signed "E. M. W. S.," and are dated July 19, 1901. The lines are:

> The voice of him I loved is still,
> The restless brain is quiet;
> The troubled heart has ceased to beat,
> And the surging blood to riot.

'I am told that the lady who wrote these lines is Mrs. Shepherd, who lives in South Australia, and who always wears a gold cross that Adam Lindsay Gordon gave her. The story is that Gordon, who felt that he could put his feelings into writing better than he could express them in speech, wrote an offer of marriage to the lady who afterwards became Mrs. Shepherd, and sent a black boy [sic] to deliver it. The black boy [sic] carried out this part of the contract, and, furthermore, waited for a letter in reply; but when he got back to Gordon's home he found the poet walking up and down "muttering wildly" (he was probably repeating some verses he had written) and becoming frightened, ran away, taking the letter with him. Gordon waited a long time, and receiving no answer to his proposal of marriage, never troubled the lady further. But she had written accepting the offer.'

Gordon as a poet

Beyond dispute Gordon is the national poet of Australia. In Victoria and South Australia nearly every family owns Gordon's *Poems*, and they are better known than any English poet's are known in England. And rightly, because Gordon is the voice of Australia. But for him, Australian literature would be less loyal than it is to the Old Country. For all Australians respect a man who was so much after their own heart; who would square up to anybody, or put a horse at anything; who loved the bush like a home, and extorted the admiration of all bushmen; who founded Australia's school of grim fatalism; who voiced Australia's code of honour.

Adam Lindsay Gordon was the national poet of Australia, not only because he was a real poet and wrote living poetry about the romantic old colonial days when Australia was in the making [*sic*], but because he was a typical example of the fine strain which gave the Australian people its greatest qualities.

***

Gordon was Byronic. He began with escapades and eccentricities of dress. From a boy he loved to use his fists, and, if he did not get into the School XI like Byron, he had won steeplechases at an age when most boys are absorbed in the sports of public schools. Like Byron, he sold his birthright for a mess of pottage. Like Byron's, the shades of gloom closed in round his manhood until he sank into an early grave. The phoenix rose from the ashes of both. And, if Gordon's fame is not as worldwide as Byron's, he has this to console him, that, while Byron's hold on his countrymen is now intellectual only, he enjoys the passionate love of Australia. He is Australia's hero as well as her poet. Perhaps no poet ever enjoyed such a personal devotion.

In England, as in Australia, he won the attention of every one by his fearlessness; and he won the affection of all who were in his immediate circle by his merry spontaneous nature. But his lightheartedness led to his sowing wild oats, and they seemed to his father so wild that he shipped him off to Australia, not, we must believe, so much with the idea of ridding himself of a nuisance, as with the idea that his son's courage and adventurousness might be turned to good account in the lawless atmosphere of the Great Gold Rush. We may think this, because he procured for him a commission for which the poet never applied, in the South Australian Mounted Police. Gordon preferred to enlist in the same corps as a constable, and from that moment the steady improvement in his character began.

Gordon had many misfortunes and hardships in Australia, but every year he grew more manly and respected, and in his last days, when he was broken by accidents and poverty, we find him the valued and intimate friend, and a favourite guest in the houses of the most prominent men in their respective colonies, like the Riddochs and the Powers.

***

Gordon's poems, which are so full of the open air in their atmosphere, were all composed out of doors. They were only copied out indoors. Some may have been jotted down on odd scraps of paper, but for a man with a verbal memory like Gordon's, it could have been no effort to compose a poem and carry it in his head for some time before he wrote it down. I have never heard if Gordon knew his own poems by heart, but he certainly knew the whole of Macaulay's *Lays of Ancient Rome* by heart; and he could spout prodigious quantities of Scott, Byron, Browning, and Swinburne – not to mention Horace, Virgil, Ovid, and Homer.

The fact stands out that these poems, which are so redolent of the bush, were written in the bush by one who made the bush his life. Their background is full of the broad effects which would have been his atmosphere to a short-sighted man who spent his life in the bush. But his bad eyesight prevented him from filling in details of the foreground. The country round Mount Gambier, with its lakes and floods, must have been full of snakes: Gordon hardly mentions them. He mentions a few trees – various gums, the wattle, the blackwood, the she-oak, the tea-tree, and the honeysuckle, but hardly any flowers except the wattle and tea-tree blossoms. He has nothing to say about the resplendent parakeets, which are gayer than the flowers in Australia, and are found there by millions, or about huge birds like the Emu, the Eaglehawk, the Wild Swan, the Pelican, the Native Companion, the Wild Turkey, and the Bustard.

A few times he mentions the Dingo or wild dog, but never, or hardly ever, the innumerable opossums, wild cats, and native bears. He has very little to say about any lizards, though they come next in numbers after the ants, and nothing about the enormous iguana. Even the corn-grower's curse, the great white cockatoo, which comes down in flocks that whiten a field and sweep it bare like locusts, hardly crosses our vision.

Gordon makes his bush effects with bushmen. He used little else except sounds, light and darkness, heat and shade.

And this method has great advantages because it makes his poems truly *dramatic lyrics*—not musings about still life—scenery or natural history, like so many forest poems, even Kendall's. The Kendall method produces the better poetry and more good writers, but the world at large will always be more interested in dramatic lyrics, and personally I think that Gordon, with his literary offspring Rudyard Kipling, stands at the very top of the tree in this form of writing. I do not, of course, claim for them the technical finish of the great masters of poetical style, but

Browning achieved his fame without any respect for perfection of metre and vocabulary, and both Gordon (who could recite Browning by the page) and Mr. Kipling have a splendid and haunting swing, and have swept into the net of poetry a miraculous draught of expressions and experiences of common life. Gordon gave the bushman and the jockey his halo of poetry; Mr. Kipling laid it on the head of Tommy Atkins (the descendant of the archers of Creçy and Poietiers), the engineer, the merchant seaman, and the flotsam of Empire. These two have put the theories of Walt Whitman into a more articulate form. They have sung in ringing ballads the struggles of the men who lead hard and dangerous lives in their everyday round. Their song is always of battle, although their battles are not always those of knights in mail, or clashing armies. They are the poets of action.

The curious feature in the matter is that Gordon, much more the classical of the two in language and subject, led a wild bush life, while Mr. Kipling has always written as an observer, not drawing on his own experiences. It is his genius which has enabled him to put himself inside the minds of his heroes. It is on him that the mantle of Gordon, the laureate of the brave, has fallen, rather than on the writers of bush ballads, who are spoken of as the school of Gordon.

***

The sources of Gordon's popularity as a poet are personality, subject, and style. Chief among them is the intense personality which vibrates through the poems. Gordon is never a Wordsworth, filling his hives steadily from all the suitable flowers round him. He never writes poems as intellectual exercises—as essays in rhyme and rhythm on phases supplied by nature or domestic incidents. His poems well up from his heart like strong springs, and sweep the reader along with them. In other words he is a *vates*, the word which the Romans applied to a great poet in all senses of the word—not only as a maker of verses, but as a prophet and a preacher who has a message to deliver. He was one of those curious vessels chosen by the Lord to stop the passer-by, and force him to take an interest in the enigma of life. That wonderful personality, so arrestee, so splendid, so tragic, must have been given him for the purpose.

Subject, of course, counted for an immense deal in Gordon's popularity. But it was not till his last days that Gordon wrote of sport consciously because people were interested in sport, and the verses he wrote under that influence, except 'Visions in the Smoke,' which may have been written already, and merely served as the sample which secured him the order for the others, are, but for their knowledge of horses and their metrical merits, among the least valuable of Gordon's poems. Up to this he had written of sport because sport was the matter that lay nearest to his hand. Like Walt Whitman, he had said [that] nothing is unsuitable for poetry which can be made a vehicle for feeling and creation.

But his magnificent 'How We Beat the Favourite,' and the ringing, manful, breezy, picturesque poetical proverbs of 'Ye Wearie Wayfarer,' belong to a very different order. Gordon wrote those because he felt Australia in his veins. I know from personal experience what this means to a young man, for I went to Australia straight from Oxford when I was little older than Gordon, and going up on stations in the western district of Victoria belonging to various connections of my family, spent months in sheer exultation over the forest primeval of the Otway, the plains that lost themselves in the horizon, the glittering Australian climate, the champagne-like air, the long days in the saddle, the shooting of extraordinary game, the flashing by of parrots and cockatoos, the hiss of the angry snake, the excitements of raging floods and raging bush-fires. And all except the climate Gordon must have felt a hundredfold. In my time we went into the forest on purpose to get the wild life, as one takes a rough shooting in the Hebrides; in Gordon's time, the whole country was only just emerging from its primeval state; the blacks [*sic*] were still a menace to solitary stations farther north, though curiously enough Gordon never alludes to raids by the blacks, and hardly alludes to the blacks at all, probably because the subject of the reprisals by the settlers was distasteful to him. In Gordon's time one had often to ride from station to station through the bush. To Adelaide itself from Mount Gambier he once rode through the ninety-mile desert. The memories of the Great Gold Rush were still fresh; the bushranger was still abroad in the land. Life was full of stimulants which were watered down by my time.

Yet I felt intoxicated with that year I spent on stations in Australia, and I had not chafed against the conditions of my life in England.

How much more, then, should Gordon, who was forever kicking against the pricks in England, have rejoiced like a young colt in the wild life of his time? What could be more natural than that his exultation should have found vent in poetry – the poetry which he met in his everyday surroundings.

It is this which makes those early sporting poems so spontaneous, so original, so irresistible,

The third element in the popularity of Gordon was the charm of the style he evolved. Gordon was familiar with the sporting verses which had been written by hunting-men in England, but, unlike most sporting men, he also loved all good poetry – Latin and Greek and French, as well as English. So he was able to improve his models. What made him better than all other sporting poets was that he was a much better poet than any of them, and that he had exactly the ear for devising and executing the ringing metres which his subjects demanded. There is no other volume of sporting poetry so dashing as Gordon's dashing in subject, style, and metre. Gordon was a genius. Kipling is the only other genius who has written English poetry in the vernacular, and he is not a sporting poet.

But Gordon was not a poet of the first order. He had not the broad humanity, the serene power of a Homer, a Chaucer, a Shakespeare, or a Longfellow. Within his range he was strong, but his range was somewhat narrow. He was, however, a true poet, as is shown by his universal and growing popularity in his own land. A poet who appeals to the lettered and the unlettered alike, who is popular with the student and popular with the stable boy, must be a true poet. A man may appeal to a class as the mouthpiece of that class; he cannot appeal to all classes alike if he be not genuine.

Gordon's 'Sick Stockrider' is the essence of the man. It displays, in a marked degree, his eloquence, his ringing rhythm, his knowledge of the bush; and it is the child of his history, the genuine outcome of his wild heart. Had he never written another piece, his fame would have been assured.

The manly melancholy of Gordon's poetry rings true.

DOUGLAS SLADEN
The Avenue House,
Richmond, Surrey,
12th August 1912.

Adam Lindsay Gordon

"A rise steeply sloping,
A fence with stone coping"
An illustration for *How We Beat the Favourite*
H. J. Woodhouse 1908
State Library of Victoria, ID1678509.

Preface

By Marcus Clarke
Author of *For the Term of His Natural Life*

The poems of Gordon have an interest beyond the mere personal one which his friends attach to his name. Written, as they were, at odd times and leisure moments of a stirring and adventurous life, it is not to be wondered at if they are unequal or unfinished. The astonishment of those who knew the man, and can gauge the capacity of this city to foster poetic instinct, is, that such work was ever produced here at all. Intensely nervous, and feeling much of that shame at the exercise of the higher intelligence which besets those who are known to be renowned in field sports, Gordon produced his poems shyly, scribbled them on scraps of paper, and sent them anonymously to magazines. It was not until he discovered one morning that everybody knew a couplet or two of 'How we Beat the Favourite' that he consented to forego his anonymity and appear in the unsuspected character of a verse maker. The success of his republished collected poems gave him courage, and the unreserved praise which greeted *Bush Ballads* should have urged him to forget or to conquer those evil promptings which, unhappily, brought about his untimely death.

Adam Lindsay Gordon was the son of an officer in the English army, and was educated at Woolwich, in order that he might follow the profession of his family. At the time when he was a cadet there was no sign of either of the two great wars which were about to call forth the strength of English arms, and, like many other men of his day, he quitted his prospects of service and emigrated. He went to South Australia and started as a sheep farmer. His efforts were attended with failure. He lost his capital and, owning nothing but a love for horsemanship and a head full of Browning and Shelley, plunged into the varied life which gold-mining, "over-landing" and cattle-driving affords. From this experience he emerged to light in Melbourne as the best amateur steeplechase rider in the colonies. The victory he won for Major Baker in 1868, when he rode Babbler for the Cup Steeplechase, made him popular, and the almost simultaneous publication of his last volume of poems gave him welcome entrance to the houses of all who had pretensions to literary taste. The reputation of the book spread to England, and Major Whyte Melville did not disdain to place the lines of the dashing Australian author at the head of his own dashing descriptions of sporting scenery.

Unhappily, the melancholy which Gordon's friends had with pain observed increased daily, and in the full flood of his success, with congratulations pouring upon him from every side, he was found dead in the heather near his home with a bullet from his own rifle in his brain.

I do not purpose to criticise the volumes which these few lines of preface introduce to the reader. The influence of Browning and of Swinburne upon the writer's taste is plain. There is plainly visible also, however, a keen sense for natural beauty and a manly admiration for healthy living. If in 'Ashtaroth' and 'Bellona' we recognise the swing of a familiar metre, in such poems as the 'Sick Stockrider' we perceive the genuine poetic instinct united to a very clear perception of the loveliness of duty and of labour.

'Twas merry in the glowing morn, among the gleaming grass,
To wander as we've wandered many a mile,
And blow the cool tobacco cloud, and watch the white wreaths pass,
Sitting loosely in the saddle all the while;

'Twas merry 'mid the blackwoods, when we spied the station roofs,
To wheel the wild scrub cattle at the yard,
With a running fire of stockwhips, and a fiery run of hoofs,
Oh! the hardest day was never then too hard!

Aye! we had a glorious gallop after "Starlight" and his gang,
When they bolted from Sylvester's on the flat;
How the sun-dried reed-beds crackled, how the flint-strewn ranges rang
To the strokes of "Mountaineer" and "Acrobat";

Hard behind them in the timber, harder still across the heath,
Close behind them through the tea-tree scrub we dash'd;

Adam Lindsay Gordon

And the golden-tinted fern leaves, how they rustled underneath!
And the honeysuckle osiers, how they crash'd!

This is genuine. There is no "poetic evolution from the depths of internal consciousness" here. The writer has ridden his ride as well as written it. The student of these unpretending volumes will be repaid for his labour. He will find in them something very like the beginnings of a national school of Australian poetry. In historic Europe, where every rood of ground is hallowed in legend and in song, the least imaginative can find food for sad and sweet reflection. When strolling at noon down an English country lane, lounging at sunset by some ruined chapel on the margin of an Irish lake, or watching the mists of morning unveil Ben Lomond, we feel all the charm which springs from association with the past. Soothed, saddened and cheered by turns, we partake of the varied moods which belong not so much to ourselves as to the dead men who, in old days, sung, suffered or conquered in the scenes which we survey. But this our native or adopted land has no past, no story.[2] No poet speaks to us. Do we need a poet to interpret Nature's teachings, we must look into our own hearts, if perchance we may find a poet there.

What is the dominant note of Australian scenery? That which is the dominant note of Edgar Allan Poe's

---

[2] Editor's note: This viewpoint regarding Australia's history is untenable, given the rich histories of Aboriginal and Torres Strait Islander peoples across the land. Of course, for Clarke, as for many of his contemporaries, 'history' here is equated with Western history.

poetry—Weird Melancholy. A poem like 'L'Allegro' could never be written by an Australian. It is too airy, too sweet, too freshly happy. The Australian mountain forests are funereal, secret, stern. Their solitude is desolation. They seem to stifle, in their black gorges, a story of sullen despair. No tender sentiment is nourished in their shade. In other lands the dying year is mourned, the falling leaves drop lightly on his bier. In the Australian forests no leaves fall. The savage winds shout among the rock clefts. From the melancholy gum, strips of white bark hang and rustle. The very animal life of these frowning hills is either grotesque or ghostly. Great grey kangaroos hop noiselessly over the coarse grass. Flights of white cockatoos stream out, shrieking like evil souls. The sun suddenly sinks, and the mopokes burst out into horrible peals of semi-human laughter. The natives [*sic*] aver that, when night comes, from out the bottomless depth of some lagoon the Bunyip rises, and, in form like monstrous sea calf, drags his loathsome length from out the ooze. From a corner of the silent forest rises a dismal chant, and around a fire dance natives painted like skeletons. All is fear-inspiring and gloomy. No bright fancies are linked with the memories of the mountains. Hopeless explorers have named them out of their sufferings Mount Misery, Mount Dreadful, Mount Despair. As when among sylvan scenes in places

> Made green with the running of rivers,
> And gracious with temperate air,

the soul is soothed and satisfied, so, placed before the frightful grandeur of these barren hills, it drinks in their sentiment of defiant ferocity, and is steeped in bitterness.

Australia has rightly been named the Land of the Dawning. Wrapped in the midst of early morning, her history looms vague and gigantic. The lonely horseman riding between the moonlight and the day sees vast shadows creeping across the shelterless and silent plains, hears strange noises in the primeval forest where flourishes a vegetation long dead in other lands, and feels, despite his fortune, that the trim utilitarian civilisation which bred him shrinks into insignificance beside the contemptuous grandeur of forest and ranges, coeval with an age in which European scientists have cradled his own race.

There is a poem in every form of tree or flower, but the poetry which lives in the trees and flowers of Australia differs from those of other countries. Europe is the home of knightly song, of bright deeds and clear morning thought. Asia sinks beneath the weighty recollections of her past magnificence, as the Suttee sinks, jewel-burdened, upon the corpse of dead grandeur, destructive even in its death. America swiftly hurries on her way, rapid, glittering, insatiable even as one of her own giant waterfalls. From the jungles of Africa, and the creeper-tangled groves of the islands of the South, arise—from the glowing hearts of a thousand flowers—heavy and intoxicating odours the Upas-poison which dwells in barbaric sensuality. In Australia alone is to be found the Grotesque, the Weird, the strange scribblings of nature learning how to write. Some see no beauty in our trees without shade, our flowers without perfume, our birds who cannot fly, and our beasts who have not yet learned to walk on all fours. But the dweller in the wilderness acknowledges the subtle charm of this fantastic land of monstrosities. He becomes familiar with the beauty of loneliness. Whispered to by the myriad tongues of the wilderness, he learns the language of the barren and the uncouth, and can read the hieroglyphs of haggard gum-trees, blown into odd shapes, distorted with fierce hot winds, or cramped with cold nights, when the Southern Cross freezes in a cloudless sky of icy blue. The phantasmagoria of that wild dreamland termed the Bush interprets itself, and the Poet of our desolation begins to comprehend why free Esau loved his heritage of desert sand better than all the bountiful richness of Egypt.

Adam Lindsay Gordon

A Dedication

To the Author of "Holmby House"[3]

They are rhymes rudely strung with intent less
    Of sound than of words,
In lands where bright blossoms are scentless,
    And songless bright birds;
Where, with fire and fierce drought on her tresses,
Insatiable Summer oppresses
Sere woodlands and sad wildernesses,
    And faint flocks and herds.

Where in dreariest days, when all dews end,
    And all winds are warm,
Wild Winter's large flood-gates are loosen'd,
    And floods, freed by storm,
From broken up fountain heads, dash on
Dry deserts with long pent up passion—
Here rhyme was first framed without fashion,
    Song shaped without form.

Whence gather'd?—The locust's glad chirrup
    May furnish a stave;
The ring of a rowel and stirrup,
    The wash of a wave.
The chaunt of the marsh frog in rushes,
That chimes through the pauses and hushes

---

[3] Major Whyte-Melville, the novelist.

Of nightfall, the torrent that gushes,
    The tempests that rave.

In the deep'ning of dawn, when it dapples
    The dusk of the sky,
With streaks like the redd'ning of apples,
    The ripening of rye.
To eastward, when cluster by cluster,
Dim stars and dull planets that muster,
Wax wan in a world of white lustre
    That spreads far and high.

In the gathering of night gloom o'erhead, in
    The still silent change,
All fire-flushed when forest trees redden
    On slopes of the range.
When the gnarl'd, knotted trunks Eucalyptian
Seem carved, like weird columns Egyptian,
With curious device—quaint inscription,
    And hieroglyph strange.

In the Spring, when the wattle gold trembles
    'Twixt shadow and shine,
When each dew-laden air draught resembles
    A long draught of wine;
When the sky-line's blue burnish'd resistance
Makes deeper the dreamiest distance,
Some song in all hearts hath existence,—
    Such songs have been mine.

Adam Lindsay Gordon

They came in all guises, some vivid
    To clasp and to keep;
Some sudden and swift as the livid
    Blue thunder-flame's leap.
This swept through the first breath of clover
With memories renew'd to the rover—
That flash'd while the black horse turn'd over
    Before the long sleep.

To you (having cunning to colour
    A page with your pen,
That through dull days, and nights even duller,
    Long years ago ten,
Fair pictures in fever afforded)—
I send these rude staves, roughly worded
By one in whose brain stands recorded
    As clear now as then,

"The great rush of grey 'Northern water',
    The green ridge of bank,
The 'sorrel' with curved sweep of quarter
    Curl'd close to clean flank,
The Royalist saddlefast squarely,
And where the bright uplands stretch fairly,
Behind, beyond pistol-shot barely,
    The Roundheaded rank.

A long launch, with clinging of muscles,
    And clenching of teeth!
The loose doublet ripples and rustles!

The swirl shoots beneath!"
Enough. In return for your garland—
In lieu of the flowers from your far land—
Take wild growth of dreamland or starland,
    Take weeds for your wreath.

Yet rhyme had not fail'd me for reason,
    Nor reason for rhyme,
Sweet Song! had I sought you in season,
    And found you in time.
You beckon in your bright beauty yonder,
And I, waxing fainter, yet fonder,
Now weary too soon when I wander—
    Now fall when I climb.

It matters but little in the long run,
    The weak have some right—
Some share in the race that the strong run,
    The fight the strong fight.
If words that are worthless go westward,
Yet the worst word shall be as the best word,
In the day when all riot sweeps restward,
    In darkness or light.

Adam Lindsay Gordon

The Sick Stockrider
Painting by Charlie Hammond, 1905.
State Library of Victoria, ID1679478.

The Sick Stockrider

Hold hard, Ned! Lift me down once more, and lay me in the shade.
Old man, you've had your work cut out to guide
Both horses, and to hold me in the saddle when I sway'd,
All through the hot, slow, sleepy, silent ride.
The dawn at "Moorabinda" was a mist rack dull and dense,
The sunrise was a sullen, sluggish lamp;
I was dozing in the gateway at Arbuthnot's bound'ry fence,
I was dreaming on the Limestone cattle camp.
We crossed the creek at Carricksford, and sharply through the haze,
And suddenly the sun shot flaming forth;
To southward lay "Katâwa", with the sandpeaks all ablaze,
And the flush'd fields of Glen Lomond lay to north.
Now westward winds the bridle path that leads to Lindisfarm,
And yonder looms the double-headed Bluff;
From the far side of the first hill, when the skies are clear and calm,
You can see Sylvester's woolshed fair enough.
Five miles we used to call it from our homestead to the place
Where the big tree spans the roadway like an arch;
'Twas here we ran the dingo down that gave us such a chase

Adam Lindsay Gordon

Eight years ago—or was it nine?—last March.

'Twas merry in the glowing morn, among the gleaming
 grass,
To wander as we've wandered many a mile,
And blow the cool tobacco cloud, and watch the white
 wreaths pass,
Sitting loosely in the saddle all the while.
'Twas merry 'mid the blackwoods, when we spied the
 station roofs,
To wheel the wild scrub cattle at the yard,
With a running fire of stockwhips and a fiery run of hoofs;
Oh! the hardest day was never then too hard!

Aye! we had a glorious gallop after "Starlight" and his
 gang,
When they bolted from Sylvester's on the flat;
How the sun-dried reed-beds crackled, how the flint-
 strewn ranges rang
To the strokes of "Mountaineer" and "Acrobat".
Hard behind them in the timber, harder still across the
 heath,
Close beside them through the tea-tree scrub we dash'd;
And the golden-tinted fern leaves, how they rustled
 underneath!
And the honeysuckle osiers, how they crash'd!

We led the hunt throughout, Ned, on the chestnut and the
 grey,
And the troopers were three hundred yards behind,

While we emptied our six-shooters on the bushrangers at bay,
In the creek with stunted box-tree for a blind!
There you grappled with the leader, man to man and horse to horse,
And you roll'd together when the chestnut rear'd;
He blazed away and missed you in that shallow watercourse—
A narrow shave—his powder singed your beard!

In these hours when life is ebbing, how those days when life was young
Come back to us; how clearly I recall
Even the yarns Jack Hall invented, and the songs Jem Roper sung;
And where are now Jem Roper and Jack Hall?

Aye! nearly all our comrades of the old colonial school,
Our ancient boon companions, Ned, are gone;
Hard livers for the most part, somewhat reckless as a rule,
It seems that you and I are left alone.

There was Hughes, who got in trouble through that business with the cards,
It matters little what became of him;
But a steer ripp'd up MacPherson in the Cooraminta yards,
And Sullivan was drown'd at Sink-or-swim;
And Mostyn—poor Frank Mostyn—died at last a fearful wreck,
In "the horrors", at the Upper Wandinong,

Adam Lindsay Gordon

And Carisbrooke, the rider, at the Horsefall broke his neck,
Faith! the wonder was he saved his neck so long!

Ah! those days and nights we squandered at the Logans' in the glen—
The Logans, man and wife, have long been dead.
Elsie's tallest girl seems taller than your little Elsie then;
And Ethel is a woman grown and wed.

I've had my share of pastime, and I've done my share of toil,
And life is short—the longest life a span;
I care not now to tarry for the corn or for the oil,
Or for the wine that maketh glad the heart of man.
For good undone and gifts misspent and resolutions vain,
'Tis somewhat late to trouble. This I know—
I should live the same life over, if I had to live again;
And the chances are I go where most men go.

The deep blue skies wax dusky, and the tall green trees grow dim,
The sward beneath me seems to heave and fall;
And sickly, smoky shadows through the sleepy sunlight swim,
And on the very sun's face weave their pall.
Let me slumber in the hollow where the wattle blossoms wave,
With never stone or rail to fence my bed;

Should the sturdy station children pull the bush flowers on my grave,
I may chance to hear them romping overhead.

Adam Lindsay Gordon

The Swimmer

With short, sharp, violent lights made vivid,
To southward far as the sight can roam;
Only the swirl of the surges livid,
The seas that climb and the surfs that comb.
Only the crag and the cliff to nor'ward,
And the rocks receding, and reefs flung forward,
And waifs wreck'd seaward and wasted shoreward
On shallows sheeted with flaming foam.

A grim, grey coast and a seaboard ghastly,
And shores trod seldom by feet of men—
Where the batter'd hull and the broken mast lie,
They have lain embedded these long years ten.
Love! when we wander'd here together,
Hand in hand through the sparkling weather,
From the heights and hollows of fern and heather,
God surely loved us a little then.

The skies were fairer and shores were firmer—
The blue sea over the bright sand roll'd;
Babble and prattle, and ripple and murmur,
Sheen of silver and glamour of gold—
And the sunset bath'd in the gulf to lend her
A garland of pinks and of purples tender,
A tinge of the sun-god's rosy splendour,
A tithe of his glories manifold.

Man's works are graven, cunning, and skilful

On earth, where his tabernacles are;
But the sea is wanton, the sea is wilful,
And who shall mend her and who shall mar?
Shall we carve success or record disaster
On the bosom of her heaving alabaster?
Will her purple pulse beat fainter or faster
For fallen sparrow or fallen star?

I would that with sleepy, soft embraces
The sea would fold me—would find me rest,
In luminous shades of her secret places,
In depths where her marvels are manifest;
So the earth beneath her should not discover
My hidden couch—nor the heaven above her—
As a strong love shielding a weary lover,
I would have her shield me with shining breast.

When light in the realms of space lay hidden,
When life was yet in the womb of time,
Ere flesh was fettered to fruits forbidden,
And souls were wedded to care and crime,
Was the course foreshaped for the future spirit—
A burden of folly, a void of merit—
That would fain the wisdom of stars inherit,
And cannot fathom the seas sublime?

Under the sea or the soil (what matter?
The sea and the soil are under the sun),
As in the former days in the latter,
The sleeping or waking is known of none.

Adam Lindsay Gordon

Surely the sleeper shall not awaken
To griefs forgotten or joys forsaken,
For the price of all things given and taken,
The sum of all things done and undone.

Shall we count offences or coin excuses,
Or weigh with scales the soul of a man,
Whom a strong hand binds and a sure hand looses,
Whose light is a spark and his life a span?
The seed he sow'd or the soil he cumber'd,
The time he served or the space he slumber'd,
Will it profit a man when his days are number'd,
Or his deeds since the days of his life began?

One, glad because of the light, saith, "Shall not
The righteous Judge of all the earth do right,
For behold the sparrows on the house-tops fall not
Save as seemeth to Him good in His sight?"
And this man's joy shall have no abiding,
Through lights departing and lives dividing,
He is soon as one in the darkness hiding,
One loving darkness rather than light.

A little season of love and laughter,
Of light and life, and pleasure and pain,
And a horror of outer darkness after,
And dust returneth to dust again.
Then the lesser life shall be as the greater,
And the lover of life shall join the hater,
And the one thing cometh sooner or later,

And no one knoweth the loss or gain.

Love of my life! we had lights in season—
Hard to part from, harder to keep—
We had strength to labour and souls to reason,
And seed to scatter and fruits to reap.
Though time estranges and fate disperses,
We have *had* our loves and our loving mercies;
Though the gifts of the light in the end are curses,
Yet bides the gift of the darkness—sleep!

See! girt with tempest and wing'd with thunder,
And clad with lightning and shod with sleet,
The strong winds treading the swift waves sunder
The flying rollers with frothy feet.
One gleam like a bloodshot sword-blade swims on
The sky-line, staining the green gulf crimson,
A death stroke fiercely dealt by a dim sun,
That strikes through his stormy winding-sheet.

Oh! brave white horses! you gather and gallop,
The storm sprite loosens the gusty reins;
Now the stoutest ship were the frailest shallop
In your hollow backs, or your high arch'd manes.
I would ride as never a man has ridden
In your sleepy, swirling surges hidden,
To gulfs foreshadow'd through straits forbidden,
Where no light wearies and no love wanes.

Adam Lindsay Gordon

From the Wreck

   Written on the bough of the old gumtree, while Gordon was staying with John Riddoch at Yallum in January 1869.

"Turn out, boys!"—"What's up with our super tonight?
The man's mad—Two hours to daybreak I'd swear—
Stark mad—why, there isn't a glimmer of light."
"Take Bolingbroke, Alec, give Jack the young mare;
Look sharp. A large vessel lies jamm'd on the reef,
And many on board still, and some wash'd on shore.
Ride straight with the news—they may send some relief
From the township; and we—we can do little more.
You, Alec, you know the near cuts; you can cross
'The Sugarloaf' ford with a scramble, I think;
Don't spare the blood filly, nor yet the black horse;
Should the wind rise, God help them! the ship will soon
   sink.
Old Peter's away down the paddock, to drive
The nags to the stockyard as fast as he can—
A life and death matter; so, lads, look alive."
Half-dress'd, in the dark, to the stockyard we ran.

There was bridling with hurry, and saddling with haste,
Confusion and cursing for lack of a moon;
"Be quick with these buckles, we've no time to waste;"
"Mind the mare, she can use her hind legs to some tune."
"Make sure of the crossing-place; strike the old track,

They've fenced off the new one; look out for the holes
On the wombat hills." "Down with the slip rails; stand
    back."
"And ride, boys, the pair of you, ride for your souls."

In the low branches heavily laden with dew,
In the long grasses spoiling with deadwood that day,
Where the blackwood, the box, and the bastard oak grew,
Between the tall gum-trees we gallop'd away—
We crash'd through a brush fence, we splash'd through a
    swamp—
We steered for the north near "The Eaglehawk's Nest"—
We bore to the left, just beyond "The Red Camp",
And round the black tea-tree belt wheel'd to the west—
We cross'd a low range sickly scented with musk
From wattle-tree blossom—we skirted a marsh—
Then the dawn faintly dappled with orange the dusk,
And peal'd overhead the jay's laughter note harsh,
And shot the first sunstreak behind us, and soon
The dim dewy uplands were dreamy with light;
And full on our left flash'd "The Reedy Lagoon",
And sharply "The Sugarloaf" rear'd on our right.
A smothered curse broke through the bushman's brown
    beard,
He turn'd in his saddle, his brick-colour'd cheek
Flush'd feebly with sundawn, said, "Just what I fear'd;
Last fortnight's late rainfall has flooded the creek."

Black Bolingbroke snorted, and stood on the brink
One instant, then deep in the dark sluggish swirl

Adam Lindsay Gordon

**"With a running fire of stockwhips,
and a fiery run of hoofs"**
Illustration for: The Sick Stockrider
H. J. Woodhouse, 1908
State Library of Victoria, ID1678515.

Plunged headlong. I saw the horse suddenly sink,
Till round the man's armpits the waves seemed to curl.
We follow'd—one cold shock, and deeper we sank
Than they did, and twice tried the landing in vain;
The third struggle won it; straight up the steep bank
We stagger'd, then out on the skirts of the plain.

The stockrider, Alec, at starting had got
The lead, and had kept it throughout; 'twas his boast
That through thickest of scrub he could steer like a shot,
And the black horse was counted the best on the coast.
The mare had been awkward enough in the dark,
She was eager and headstrong, and barely half broke;
She had had me too close to a big stringy-bark,
And had made a near thing of a crooked sheoak;
But now on the open, lit up by the morn,
She flung the white foam-flakes from nostril to neck,
And chased him—I hatless, with shirt sleeves all torn
(For he may ride ragged who rides from a wreck)—
And faster and faster across the wide heath
We rode till we raced. Then I gave her her head,
And she—stretching out with the bit in her teeth—
She caught him, outpaced him, and passed him, and led.

We neared the new fence, we were wide of the track;
I look'd right and left—she had never been tried
At a stiff leap; 'twas little he cared on the black.
"You're more than a mile from the gateway," he cried.
I hung to her head, touched her flank with the spurs
(In the red streak of rail not the ghost of a gap);

Adam Lindsay Gordon

She shortened her long stroke, she pricked her sharp ears,
She flung it behind her with hardly a rap—
I saw the post quiver where Bolingbroke struck,
And guessed that the pace we had come the last mile
Had blown him a bit (he could jump like a buck).
We galloped more steadily then for a while.

The heath was soon pass'd, in the dim distance lay
The mountain. The sun was just clearing the tips
Of the ranges to eastward. The mare—could she stay?
She was bred very nearly as clean as Eclipse;
She led, and as oft as he came to her side,
She took the bit free and untiring as yet;
Her neck was arched double, her nostrils were wide,
And the tips of her tapering ears nearly met—
"You're lighter than I am," said Alec at last;
"The horse is dead beat and the mare isn't blown.
She must be a good one—ride on and ride fast,
You know your way now." So I rode on alone.

Still galloping forward we pass'd the two flocks
At McIntyre's hut and McAllister's hill—
She was galloping strong at the Warrigal Rocks—
On the Wallaby Range she was galloping still—
And over the wasteland and under the wood,
By down and by dale, and by fell and by flat,
She gallop'd, and here in the stirrups I stood
To ease her, and there in the saddle I sat
To steer her. We suddenly struck the red loam
Of the track near the troughs, then she reeled on the rise—

From her crest to her croup covered over with foam,
And blood-red her nostrils, and bloodshot her eyes,
A dip in the dell where the wattle fire bloomed—
A bend round a bank that had shut out the view—
Large framed in the mild light the mountain had loomed,
With a tall, purple peak bursting out from the blue.

I pull'd her together, I press'd her, and she
Shot down the decline to the Company's yard,
And on by the paddocks, yet under my knee
I could feel her heart thumping the saddle-flaps hard.
Yet a mile and another, and now we were near
The goal, and the fields and the farms flitted past;
And 'twixt the two fences I turned with a cheer,
For a green grass-fed mare 'twas a far thing and fast;
And labourers, roused by her galloping hoofs,
Saw bare-headed rider and foam-sheeted steed;
And shone the white walls and the slate-coloured roofs
Of the township. I steadied her then—I had need—
Where stood the old chapel (where stands the new church

—

Since chapels to churches have changed in that town).
A short, sidelong stagger, a long, forward lurch,
A slight, choking sob, and the mare had gone down.
I slipp'd off the bridle, I slacken'd the girth,
I ran on and left her and told them my news;
I saw her soon afterwards. What was she worth?
How much for her hide? She had never worn shoes.

Adam Lindsay Gordon

No Name

"A stone upon her heart and head,
But no name written on that stone;
Sweet neighbours whisper low instead,
This sinner was a loving one."

—Mrs. Browning[4]

'Tis a nameless stone that stands at your head—
The gusts in the gloomy gorges whirl,
Brown leaves and red till they cover your bed—
Now I trust that your sleep is a sound one, girl!

I said in my wrath, when his shadow cross'd
From your garden gate to your cottage door,
"What does it matter for one soul lost?
Millions of souls have been lost before."

Yet I warn'd you—ah! but my words came true—
"Perhaps some day you will find him out."
He who was not worthy to loosen your shoe,
Does his conscience therefore prick him? I doubt.

You laughed and were deaf to my warning voice—
Blush'd and were blind to his cloven hoof—
You have had your chance, you have taken your choice
How could I help you, standing aloof?

---

[4] Elizabeth Barrett Browning. The citation is from the poem, "A Year's Spinning" (published 1846).

He has prosper'd well with the world—he says
I am mad—if so, and if he be sane,
I, at least, give God thanksgiving and praise
That there lies between us one difference plain.

You in your beauty above me bent
In the pause of a wild west country ball—
Spoke to me—touched me without intent—
Made me your servant for once and all.

Light laughter rippled your rose-red lip,
And you swept my cheek with a shining curl,
That stray'd from your shoulder's snowy tip—
Now I pray that your sleep is a sound one, girl!

From a long way off to look at your charms
Made my blood run redder in every vein,
And he—he has held you long in his arms,
And has kiss'd you over and over again.

Is it well that he keeps well out of my way?
If we met, he and I—we alone—we two—
Would I give him one moment's grace to pray?
Not I, for the sake of the soul he slew.

A life like a shuttlecock may be toss'd
With the hand of fate for a battledore;
But it matters much for your sweet soul lost,
As much as a million souls and more.

Adam Lindsay Gordon

And I know that if, here or there, alone,
I found him, fairly and face to face,
Having slain his body, I would slay my own,
That my soul to Satan his soul might chase.

He hardens his heart in the public way—
Who am I? I am but a nameless churl;
But God will put all things straight some day—
Till then may your sleep be a sound one, girl!

Adam Lindsay Gordon – Melbourne monument. Sculpted by Paul Raphael Montford. Photo by VirtualSteve, 27 Dec 2006. GNU Free Doc. License.

Adam Lindsay Gordon

Wolf and Hound

Written on the bough of the old gumtree, while Gordon was staying with John Riddoch at Yallum in January 1869.

> *"The hills like giants at a hunting lay*
> *Chin upon hand, to see the game at bay."*
> —Robert Browning[5]

You'll take my tale with a little salt,
But it needs none, nevertheless,
I was foil'd completely, fairly at fault,
Dishearten'd, too, I confess.
At the splitters' tent I had seen the track
Of horse-hoofs fresh on the sward,
And though Darby Lynch and Donovan Jack
(Who could swear through a ten-inch board)
Solemnly swore he had not been there,
I was just as sure that they lied,
For to Darby all that is foul was fair,
And Jack for his life was tried.

We had run him for seven miles and more
As hard as our nags could split;
At the start they were all too weary and sore,

---

[5] From the poem, "Childe Roland to the Dark Tower Came", published in Browning's poetry collection, *Men and Women* (published 1855).

And his was quite fresh and fit.
Young Marsden's pony had had enough
On the plain, where the chase was hot;
We breasted the swell of the Bittern's Bluff,
And Mark couldn't raise a trot;
When the sea, like a splendid silver shield,
To the south-west suddenly lay;
On the brow of the Beetle the chestnut reel'd,
And I bid good-bye to McCrea—
And I was alone when the mare fell lame,
With a pointed flint in her shoe,
On the Stony Flats: I had lost the game,
And what was a man to do?

I turned away with no fixed intent
And headed for Hawthorndell;
I could neither eat in the splitters' tent,
Nor drink at the splitters' well;
I knew that they gloried in my mishap,
And I cursed them between my teeth—
A blood-red sunset through Brayton's Gap
Flung a lurid fire on the heath.

Could I reach the Dell? I had little reck,
And with scarce a choice of my own
I threw the reins on Miladi's neck—
I had freed her foot from the stone.
That season most of the swamps were dry,
And after so hard a burst,
In the sultry noon of so hot a sky,

Adam Lindsay Gordon

She was keen to appease her thirst—
Or by instinct urged or impelled by fate—
I care not to solve these things—
Certain it is that she took me straight
To the Warrigal water springs.

I can shut my eyes and recall the ground
As though it were yesterday—
With a shelf of the low, grey rocks girt round,
The springs in their basin lay;
Woods to the east and wolds to the north
In the sundown sullenly bloom'd;
Dead black on a curtain of crimson cloth
Large peaks to the westward loomed.
I led Miladi through weed and sedge,
She leisurely drank her fill;
There was something close to the water's edge,
And my heart with one leap stood still,
For a horse's shoe and a rider's boot
Had left clean prints on the clay;
Someone had watered his beast on foot.
'Twas he—he had gone. Which way?
Then the mouth of the cavern faced me fair,
As I turned and fronted the rocks;
So, at last, I had pressed the wolf to his lair,
I had run to his earth the fox.

I thought so. Perhaps he was resting. Perhaps
He was waiting, watching for me.
I examined all my revolver caps,

I hitched my mare to a tree—
I had sworn to have him, alive or dead,
And to give him a chance was loth.
He knew his life had been forfeited—
He had even heard of my oath.
In my stocking soles to the shelf I crept,
I crawl'd safe into the cave—
All silent—if he was there he slept
Not there. All dark as the grave.

Through the crack I could hear the leaden hiss!
See the livid face through the flame!
How strange it seems that a man should miss
When his life depends on his aim!
There couldn't have been a better light
For him, nor a worse for me.
We were coop'd up, caged like beasts for a fight,
And dumb as dumb beasts were we.

Flash! flash! bang! bang! and we blazed away,
And the grey roof reddened and rang;
Flash! flash! and I felt his bullet flay
The tip of my ear. Flash! bang!
Bang! flash! and my pistol arm fell broke;
I struck with my left hand then—
Struck at a corpse through a cloud of smoke—
I had shot him dead in his den!

Adam Lindsay Gordon

De Te

A burning glass of burnished brass,
The calm sea caught the noontide rays,
And sunny slopes of golden grass
And wastes of weed-flower seem to blaze.
Beyond the shining silver-greys,
Beyond the shades of denser bloom,
The skyline girt with glowing haze
The farthest, faintest forest gloom,
And the everlasting hills that loom.

We heard the hound beneath the mound,
We scared the swamp hawk hovering nigh—
We had not sought for that we found—
He lay as dead men only lie,
With wan cheek whitening in the sky,
Through the wild heath flowers, white and red,
The dumb brute that had seen him die,
Close crouching, howl'd beside the head,
Brute burial service o'er the dead.

The brow was rife with seams of strife—
A lawless death made doubly plain
The ravage of a reckless life;
The havoc of a hurricane
Of passions through that breadth of brain,
Like headlong horses that had run
Riot, regardless of the rein—

"Madman, he might have lived and done
Better than most men," whispered one.

The beams and blots that Heaven allots
To every life with life begin.
Fool! would you change the leopard's spots,
Or blanch the Ethiopian's skin?
What more could he have hoped to win,
What better things have thought to gain,
So shapen—so conceived in sin?
No life is wholly void and vain,
Just and unjust share sun and rain.

Were new life sent, and life misspent,
Wiped out (if such to God seemed good),
Would he (being as he was) repent,
Or could he, even if he would,
Who heeded not things understood
(Though dimly) even in savage lands
By some who worship stone or wood,
Or bird or beast, or who stretch hands
Sunward on shining Eastern sands?

And crime has cause. Nay, never pause
Idly to feel a pulseless wrist;
Brace up the massive, square-shaped jaws,
Unclench the stubborn, stiff'ning fist,
And close those eyes through film and mist
That kept the old defiant glare;
And answer, wise Psychologist,

Adam Lindsay Gordon

Whose science claims some little share
Of truth, what better things lay there?

Aye! thought and mind were there,—some kind
Of faculty that men mistake
For talent when their wits are blind,—
An aptitude to mar and break
What others diligently make.
This was the worst and best of him—
Wise with the cunning of the snake,
Brave with the she wolf's courage grim,
Dying hard and dumb, torn limb from limb.

And you, Brown, you're a doctor; cure
You can't, but you can kill, and he—
"*Witness his mark*"—he signed last year,
And now he signs John Smith, J.P.
We'll hold our inquest *now*, we three;
I'll be your coroner for once;
I think old Oswald ought to be
Our foreman—Jones is such a dunce,—
There's more brain in the bloodhound's sconce.

No man may shirk the allotted work,
The deed to do, the death to die;
At least I think so,—neither Turk,
Nor Jew, nor infidel am I,—
And yet I wonder when I try
To solve one question, may or must,
And shall I solve it by-and-by,

Beyond the dark, beneath the dust?
I trust so, and I only trust.

Aye, what they will, such trifles kill.
Comrade, for one good deed of yours,
Your history shall not help to fill
The mouths of many brainless boors.
It may be death absolves or cures
The sin of life. 'Twere hazardous
To assert so. If the sin endures,
Say only, "God, who has judged him thus,
Be merciful to him and us."

Adam Lindsay Gordon

How We Beat the Favourite

Written on the bough of the old gumtree, while Gordon was staying with John Riddoch at Yallum in January 1869.

A Lay of the Loamshire Hunt Cup

"Aye, squire," said Stevens, "they back him at evens;
The race is all over, bar shouting, they say;
The Clown ought to beat her; Dick Neville is sweeter
Than ever—he swears he can win all the way.

"A gentleman rider—well, I'm an outsider,
But if he's a gent who the mischief's a jock?
You swells mostly blunder, Dick rides for the plunder,
He rides, too, like thunder—he sits like a rock.

"He calls 'hunted fairly' a horse that has barely
Been stripp'd for a trot within sight of the hounds,
A horse that at Warwick beat Birdlime and Yorick,
And gave Abdelkader at Aintree nine pounds.

"They say we have no test to warrant a protest;
Dick rides for a lord and stands in with a steward;
The light of their faces they show him—his case is
Prejudged and his verdict already secured.

"But none can outlast her, and few travel faster,

She strides in her work clean away from The Drag;
You hold her and sit her, she couldn't be fitter,
Whenever you hit her she'll spring like a stag.

"And p'rhaps the green jacket, at odds though they back it,
May fall, or there's no knowing what may turn up;
The mare is quite ready, sit still and ride steady,
Keep cool; and I think you may just win the Cup."

Dark-brown with tan muzzle, just stripped for the tussle,
Stood Iseult, arching her neck to the curb,
A lean head and fiery, strong quarters and wiry,
A loin rather light, but a shoulder superb.

Some parting injunction, bestowed with great unction,
I tried to recall, but forgot like a dunce,
When Reginald Murray, full tilt on White Surrey,
Came down in a hurry to start us at once.

"Keep back in the yellow! Come up on Othello!
Hold hard on the chestnut! Turn round on The Drag!
Keep back there on Spartan! Back you, sir, in tartan!
So, steady there, easy!" and down went the flag.

We started, and Kerr made strong running on Mermaid,
Through furrows that led to the first stake-and-bound,
The crack, half extended, look'd bloodlike and splendid,
Held wide on the right where the headland was sound.

I pulled hard to baffle her rush with the snaffle,

Adam Lindsay Gordon

Before her two-thirds of the field got away,
All through the wet pasture where floods of the last year
Still loitered, they clotted my crimson with clay.

The fourth fence, a wattle, floor'd Monk and Bluebottle;
The Drag came to grief at the blackthorn and ditch,
The rails toppled over Redoubt and Red Rover,
The lane stopped Lycurgus and Leicestershire Witch.

She passed like an arrow Kildare and Cock Sparrow,
And Mantrap and Mermaid refused the stone wall;
And Giles on The Greyling came down at the paling,
And I was left sailing in front of them all.

I took them a burster, nor eased her nor nursed her
Until the Black Bullfinch led into the plough,
And through the strong bramble we bored with a scramble
—
My cap was knock'd off by the hazel-tree bough.

Where furrows looked lighter I drew the rein tighter—
Her dark chest all dappled with flakes of white foam,
Her flanks mud-bespattered, a weak rail she shattered—
We landed on turf with our heads turn'd for home.

Then crash'd a low binder, and then close behind her
The sward to the strokes of the favourite shook;
His rush roused her mettle, yet ever so little
She shortened her stride as we raced at the brook.

She rose when I hit her. I saw the stream glitter,
A wide scarlet nostril flashed close to my knee,
Between sky and water The Clown came and caught her,
The space that he cleared was a caution to see.

And forcing the running, discarding all cunning,
A length to the front went the rider in green;
A long strip of stubble, and then the big double,
Two stiff flights of rails with a quickset between.

She raced at the rasper, I felt my knees grasp her,
I found my hands give to her strain on the bit;
She rose when The Clown did—our silks as we bounded
Brush'd lightly, our stirrups clash'd loud as we lit.

A rise steeply sloping, a fence with stone coping—
The last—we diverged round the base of the hill;
His path was the nearer, his leap was the clearer,
I flogg'd up the straight, and he led sitting still.

She came to his quarter, and on still I brought her,
And up to his girth, to his breastplate she drew;
A short prayer from Neville just reach'd me, "The devil!"
He mutter'd—lock'd level the hurdles we flew.

A hum of hoarse cheering, a dense crowd careering,
All sights seen obscurely, all shouts vaguely heard;
"The green wins!" "The crimson!" The multitude swims on,
And figures are blended and features are blurr'd.

Adam Lindsay Gordon

"The horse is her master!" "The green forges past her!"
"The Clown will outlast her!" "The Clown wins!" "The
    Clown!"
The white railing races with all the white faces,
The chestnut outpaces, outstretches the brown.

On still past the gateway she strains in the straightway,
Still struggles, "The Clown by a short neck at most,"
He swerves, the green scourges, the stand rocks and
    surges,
And flashes, and verges, and flits the white post.

Aye! so ends the tussle,—I knew the tan muzzle
Was first, though the ring-men were yelling "Dead heat!"
A nose I could swear by, but Clarke said, "The mare by
A short head." And that's how the favourite was beat.

Bush Ballads

**Adam Lindsay Gordon riding at
Dowling Forest Racetrack, Ballarat**
Painting by T. H. Lyttleton, 1869
State Library of Victoria, ID1654557.

Adam Lindsay Gordon

Fragmentary Scenes from the Road to Avernus

An Unpublished Dramatic Lyric

SCENE I: "Discontent"
LAURENCE RABY

Laurence:
I said to young Allan McIlveray,
Beside the swift swirls of the North,
When, in lilac shot through with a silver ray,
We haul'd the strong salmon fish forth—
Said only, "He gave us some trouble
To land him, and what does he weigh?
Our friend has caught one that weighs double,
The game for the candle won't pay
Us to-day,
We may tie up our rods and away."

I said to old Norman McGregor,
Three leagues to the west of Glen Dhu—
I had drawn, with a touch of the trigger,
The best *bead* that ever I drew—
Said merely, "For birds in the stubble
I once had an eye—I could swear
He's down—but he's not worth the trouble

Of seeking. You once shot a bear
In his lair—
'Tis only a buck that lies there."

I said to Lord Charles only last year,
The time that we topp'd the oak rail
Between Wharton's plough and Whynne's pasture,
And clear'd the big brook in Blakesvale—
We only—at Warburton's double
He fell, then I finish'd the run
And kill'd clean—said, "So bursts a bubble
That shone half an hour in the sun—
What is won?
Your sire clear'd and captured a gun."

I said to myself, in true sorrow,
I said yestere'en, "A fair prize
Is won, and it may be to-morrow
'Twill not seem so fair in thine eyes—
Real life is a race through sore trouble,
That gains not an inch on the goal,
And bliss an intangible bubble
That cheats an unsatisfied soul,
And the whole
Of the rest an illegible scroll."

Adam Lindsay Gordon

SCENE I: "Two Exhortations"

A shooting-box in the West of Ireland. A Bedchamber. Night.

LAURENCE RABY *and* MELCHIOR.

Melchior:
Surely in the great beginning God made all things good, and still
That soul-sickness men call sinning entered not without His will.
Nay, our wisest have asserted that, as shade enhances light,
Evil is but good perverted, wrong is but the foil of right.
Banish sickness, then you banish joy for health to all that live;
Slay all sin, all good must vanish, good being but comparative.
Sophistry, you say—yet listen: look you skyward, there 'tis known
Worlds on worlds in myriads glisten—larger, lovelier than our own—
This has been, and this still shall be, here as there, in sun or star;
These things are to be and will be, those things were to be and are.
Man in man's imperfect nature is by imperfection taught:
Add one cubit to your stature if you can by taking thought.

Laurence:

Thus you would not teach that peasant, though he calls you "father".

Melchior:
True,
I should magnify this present, mystify that future, too—
We adapt our conversation always to our hearer's light.

Laurence:
I am not of your persuasion.

Melchior:
Yet the difference is but slight.

Laurence:
I, *even I*, say, "He who barters worldly weal for heavenly worth
He does well"—your saints and martyrs were examples here on earth.

Melchior:
Aye, in earlier Christian ages, while the heathen empire stood,
When the war 'twixt saints and sages cried aloud for saintly blood,
Christ was then their model truly. Now, if all were meek and pure,
Save the ungodly and the unruly, would the Christian Church endure?

Shall the toiler or the fighter dream by day and watch by
 night,
Turn the left cheek to the smiter, smitten rudely on the
 right?
Strong men must encounter bad men; so-called saints of
 latter days
Have been mostly pious madmen, lusting after righteous
 praise—
Or the thralls of superstition, doubtless worthy some
 reward,
Since they came by their condition hardly of their free
 accord.
'Tis but madness, sad and solemn, that these fakir-
 Christians feel—
Saint Stylites on his column gratified a morbid zeal.

Laurence:
By your showing, good is really on a par (of worth) with
 ill.

Melchior:
Nay, I said not so; I merely tell you both some ends fulfil
—
Priestly vows were my vocation, fast and vigil wait for
 me.
You must work and face temptation. Never should the
 strong man flee,
Though God wills the inclination with the soul at war to
 be. [*Pauses.*]

In the strife 'twixt flesh and spirit, while you can the spirit aid,
Should you fall not less your merit, be not for a fall afraid.
Whatsoe'er most right, most fit is you shall do. When all is done
Chaunt the noble *Nunc Dimittis—Benedicimur*, my son.

[Exit MELCHIOR.]

Laurence [alone]:
Why do I provoke these wrangles? Melchior talks (as well he may)
With the tongues of men and angels.
[*Takes up a pamphlet.*] What has this man got to say?
[*Reads.*] *Sic sacerdos fatur (ejus nomen quondam erat Burgo.)*
Mala mens est, caro pejus, anima infirma, ergo
I nunc, ora, sine mora—orat etiam Sancta Virgo.
[*Thinks.*]
[*Speaks.*] So it seems they mean to make her wed the usurer, Nathan Lee.
Poor Estelle! her friends forsake her; what has this to do with me?
Glad I am, at least, that Helen still refuses to discard
Her, through tales false gossips tell
in spite or heedlessness.—'Tis hard!—
Lee, the Levite!—some few years back Herbert horsewhipp'd him—the cur
Show'd his teeth and laid his ears back. Now his wealth has purchased her.

Must his baseness mar her brightness? Shall the callous, cunning churl
Revel in the rosy whiteness of that golden-headed girl?
[*Thinks and smokes.*]
[*Reads.*] *Cito certe venit vitae finis (sic sacerdos fatur),*
Nunc audite omnes, ite, vobis fabula narratur
Nunc orate et laudate, laudat etiam Alma Mater.
[*Muses.*] Such has been, and such shall still be,
here as there, in sun or star;
These things are to be and will be, those things were to be and are.
If I thought that speech worth heeding I should—Nay, it seems to me
More like Satan's special pleading than like *Gloria Domine.*
[*Lies down on his couch.*]
[*Reads.*] *Et tuquoque frater meus facta mala quod fecisti*
Denique confundit Deus omnes res quas tetegisti.
Nunc si unquam, nunc aut nunquam, sanguine adjuro Christi.

SCENE IX: "In the Garden"

Aylmer's Garden, near the Lake.
LAURENCE RABY *and* ESTELLE.

Laurence:
Come to the bank where the boat is moor'd to the willow-tree low;
Bertha, the baby, won't notice; Brian, the blockhead, won't know.

Estelle:
Bertha is not such a baby, sir, as you seem to suppose;
Brian, a blockhead he may be, more than you think—for he knows.

Laurence:
This much, at least, of your brother, from the beginning he knew
Somewhat concerning that other made such a fool of by you.

Estelle:
Firmer those bonds were and faster, Frank was my spaniel, my slave.
You! you would fain be my master; mark you! the difference is grave.

Laurence:
Call me your spaniel, your starling; take me and treat me as these,

Adam Lindsay Gordon

I would be anything, darling! aye, whatsoever you please.
Brian and Basil are "punting", leave them their dice and
 their wine,
Bertha is butterfly hunting, surely one hour shall be mine.
See, I have done with all duty; see, I can dare all disgrace,
Only to look at your beauty, feasting my eyes on your
 face.

Estelle:
Look at me, aye, till your eyes ache! How, let me ask, will
 it end?
Neither for your sake, nor my sake, but for the sake of my
 friend?

Laurence:
Is she your friend then? I own it, this is all wrong, and the
 rest,
Frustra sed anima monet, caro quod fortius est.

Estelle::
Not quite so close, Laurence Raby, not with your arm
 round my waist;
Something to look at I may be, nothing to touch or to taste.

Laurence:
Wilful as ever and wayward; why did you tempt me,
 Estelle?

Estelle:

You misinterpret each stray word, you for each inch take an ell.
Lightly all laws and ties trammel me, I am warn'd for all that.

Laurence:
[*Aside.*] Perhaps she will swallow her camel when she has strained at her gnat.

Estelle:
Therefore take thought and consider, weigh well, as I do, the whole,
You for mere beauty a bidder, say, would you barter a soul?

Laurence:
Girl! *That may* happen, but *this is*; after this welcome the worst;
Blest for one hour by your kisses, let me be evermore curs'd.
Talk not of ties to me reckless, here every tie I discard—
Make me your girdle, your necklace—

Estelle:
Laurence, you kiss me too hard.

Laurence:
Aye, 'tis the road to Avernus, *n'est ce pas vrai donc, ma belle?*

There let them bind us or burn us, *mais le jeu vaut la chandelle.*
Am I your lord or your vassal? Are you my sun or my torch?
You, when I look at you, dazzle; yet when I touch you, you scorch.

Estelle:
Yonder are Brian and Basil watching us fools from the porch.

SCENE X: "After the Quarrel"

Laurence Raby's Chamber. LAURENCE *enters, a little the worse for liquor.*

Laurence:
He never gave me a chance to speak,
And he call'd her—worse than a dog—
The girl stood up with a crimson cheek,
And I fell'd him there like a log.

I can feel the blow on my knuckles yet—
He feels it more on his brow.
In a thousand years we shall all forget
The things that trouble us now.

Adam Lindsay Gordon

SCENE XI: "Ten Paces Off"

An open country. LAURENCE *and* FORREST, BRIAN AYLMER *and* PRESCOT.

Forrest:
I've won the two tosses from Prescot;
Now hear me, and hearken and heed,
And pull that vile flower from your waistcoat,
And throw down that beast of a weed;
I'm going to give you the signal
I gave Harry Hunt at Boulogne,
The morning he met Major Bignell,
And shot him as dead as a stone;
For he must look round on his right hand
To watch the white flutter—that stops
His aim, for it takes off his sight, and
I cough while the handkerchief drops.
And you keep both eyes on his figure,
Old fellow, and don't take them off.
You've got the sawhandled hair trigger—
You sight him and shoot when I cough.

Laurence [*aside*]:
Though God will never forgive me,
Though men make light of my name,
Though my sin and my shame outlive me,
I shall not outlast my shame.
The coward, does he mean to miss me?
His right hand shakes like a leaf;

Shall I live for my friends to hiss me,
Of fools and of knaves the chief?
Shall I live for my foes to twit me?
He has master'd his nerve again—
He is firm, he will surely hit me—
Will he reach the heart or the brain?
One long look eastward and northward—
One prayer—"Our Father which art"—
And the cough chimes in with the fourth word,
And I shoot skyward—the heart.

Adam Lindsay Gordon

LAST SCENE: "Exeunt"
Helen Raby.

Helen:
Where the grave-deeps rot, where the grave-dews rust,
They dug, crying, "Earth to earth"—
Crying, "Ashes to ashes and dust to dust"—
And what are my poor prayers worth?
Upon whom shall I call, or in whom shall I trust,
Though death were indeed new birth.

And they bid me be glad for my baby's sake
That she suffered sinless and young—
Would they have me be glad when my breasts still ache
Where that small, soft, sweet mouth clung?
I am glad that the heart will so surely break
That has been so bitterly wrung.

He was false, they tell me, and what if he were?
I can only shudder and pray,
Pouring out my soul in a passionate prayer
For the soul that he cast away;
Was there nothing that once was created fair
In the potter's perishing clay?

Is it well for the sinner that souls endure?
For the sinless soul is it well?
Does the pure child lisp to the angels pure?
And where does the strong man dwell,
If the sad assurance of priests be sure,

Or the tale that our preachers tell?

The unclean has follow'd the undefiled,
And the ill *may* regain the good,
And the man *may* be even as the little child!
We are children lost in the wood—
Lord! lead us out of this tangled wild,
Where the wise and the prudent have been beguil'd,
And only the babes have stood.

Adam Lindsay Gordon Cottage,
Botanical Gardens, Ballarat VIC
Photo by Rose Stereograph Co.,
ca.1920–1954.
State Library of Victoria, ID 1766075.

Doubtful Dreams

Published in the *Colonial Monthly*, December 1868

Aye! Snows are rife in December,
And sheaves are in August yet,
And you would have me remember,
And I would rather forget;
In the bloom of the May-day weather,
In the blight of October chill,
We were dreamers of old together,—
As of old, are you dreaming still?

For nothing on earth is sadder
Than the dream that cheated the grasp,
The flower that turned to the adder,
The fruit that changed to the asp;
When the day spring in darkness closes,
As the sunset fades from the hills,
With the fragrance of perish'd roses,
With the music of parch'd-up rills.

When the sands on the sea-shore nourish
Red clover and yellow corn;
When figs on the thistle flourish,
And grapes grow thick on the thorn;
When the dead branch, blighted and blasted,
Puts forth green leaves in the spring,
Then the dream that life has outlasted

Adam Lindsay Gordon

Dead comfort to life may bring.

I have changed the soil and the season,
But whether skies freeze or flame,
The soil they flame on or freeze on
Is changed in little save name;
The loadstone points to the nor'ward,
The river runs to the sea;
And you would have me look forward,
And backward I fain would flee.

I remember the bright spring garlands,
The gold that spangled the green,
And the purple on fairy far lands,
And the white and the red bloom, seen
From the spot where we last lay dreaming
Together—yourself and I—
The soft grass beneath us gleaming,
Above us the great grave sky.

And we spoke thus: "Though we have trodden
Rough paths in our boyish years;
And some with our sweat are sodden,
And some are salt with our tears;
Though we stumble still, walking blindly,
Our paths shall be made all straight;
We are weak, but the heavens are kindly,
The skies are compassionate."

Is the clime of the old land younger,

Where the young dreams longer are nursed?
With the old insatiable hunger,
With the old unquenchable thirst,
Are you longing, as in the old years
We have longed so often in vain;
Fellow-toilers still, fellow-soldiers,
Though the seas have sundered us twain?

But the young dreams surely have faded!
Young dreams!—old dreams of young days—
Shall the new dream vex us as they did?
Or as things worth censure or praise?
Real toil is ours, real trouble,
Dim dreams of pleasure and pride;
Let the dreams disperse like a bubble,
So the toil like a dream subside.

Vain toil! Men better and braver
Rose early and rested late,
Whose burdens than ours were graver,
And sterner than ours their hate.
What fair reward had Achilles?
What rest could Alcides win?
Vain toil!"Consider the lilies,
They toil not neither do spin."

Nor for mortal toiling nor spinning
Will the matters of mortals mend;
As it was so in the beginning,
It shall be so in the end.

Adam Lindsay Gordon

The web that the weavers weave ill
Shall not be woven aright
Till the good is brought forth from evil,
As day is brought forth from night.

Vain dreams! For our fathers cherish'd
High hopes in the days that were;
And these men wonder'd and perish'd,
Nor better than these we fare;
And our due at last is their due,
They fought against odds and fell;
"En avant, les enfants perdus!"
We fight against odds as well.

The skies! Will the great skies care for
Our footsteps, straighten our path,
Or strengthen our weakness? Wherefore?
We have rather incurr'd their wrath;
When against the Captain of Hazor
The stars in their courses fought,
Did the skies shed merciful rays, or
With love was the sunshine fraught?

Can they favour man? Can they wrong man?
The unapproachable skies?
Though these gave strength to the strong man,
And wisdom gave to the wise;
When strength is turn'd to derision,
And wisdom brought to dismay,
Shall we wake from a troubled vision,

Or rest from a toilsome day?

Nay! I cannot tell. Peradventure
Our very toil is a dream,
And the works that we praise or censure,
It may be, they only seem.
If so, I would fain awaken,
Or sleep more soundly than so,
Or by dreamless sleep overtaken,
The dream I would fain forego.

For the great things of earth are small things,
The longest life is a span,
And there is an end to all things,
A season to every man,
Whose glory is dust and ashes,
Whose spirit is but a spark,
That out from the darkness flashes,
And flickers out in the dark.

We remember the pangs that wrung us
When some went down to the pit,
Who faded as leaves among us,
Who flitted as shadows flit;
What visions under the stone lie?
What dreams in the shroud sleep dwell?
For we saw the earth pit only,
And we heard only the knell.

We know not whether they slumber

Adam Lindsay Gordon

Who waken on earth no more,
As the stars of the heights in number,
As sands on the deep sea-shore.
Shall stiffness bind them, and starkness
Enthral them, by field and flood,
Till "the sun shall be turn'd to darkness,
And the moon shall be turn'd to blood."

We know not!—worse may enthral men—
"The wages of sin are death";
And so death passed upon all men,
For sin was born with man's breath.
Then the labourer spent with sinning,
His hire with his life shall spend;
For it was so in the beginning,
And shall be so in the end.

There is life in the blacken'd ember
While a spark is smouldering yet;
In a dream e'en now I remember
That dream I had lief forget—
I had lief forget, I had e'en lief
That dream with *this* doubt should die—
"If we did these things in the green leaf,
What shall be done in the dry?"

The Rhyme of Joyous Garde

Through the lattice rushes the south wind, dense
With fumes of the flowery frankincense
From hawthorn blossoming thickly;
And gold is shower'd on grass unshorn,
And poppy-fire on shuddering corn,
With May-dew flooded and flush'd with morn,
And scented with sweetness sickly.

The bloom and brilliance of summer days,
The buds that brighten, the fields that blaze,
The fruits that ripen and redden,
And all the gifts of a God-sent light
Are sadder things in my shameful sight
Than the blackest gloom of the bitterest night,
When the senses darken and deaden.

For the days recall what the nights efface,
Scenes of glory and seasons of grace,
For which there is no returning—
Else the days were even as the nights to me,
Now the axe is laid to the root of the tree,
And to-morrow the barren trunk may be
Cut down—cast forth for the burning.

Would God I had died the death that day
When the bishop blessed us before the fray
At the shrine of the Saviour's Mother;

Adam Lindsay Gordon

We buckled the spur, we braced the belt,
Arthur and I—together we knelt,
And the grasp of his kingly hand I felt
As the grasp of an only brother.

The body and the blood of Christ we shared,
Knees bended and heads bow'd down and bared,
We listened throughout the praying.
Eftsoon the shock of the foe we bore,
Shoulder to shoulder on Severn's shore,
Till our hilts were glued to our hands with gore,
And our sinews slacken'd with slaying.

Was I far from Thy Kingdom, gracious Lord,
With a shattered casque and a shiver'd sword,
On the threshold of Mary's chapel?
Pardie! I had well-nigh won that crown
Which endureth more than a knight's renown,
When the pagan giant had got me down,
Sore spent in the deadly grapple.

May his craven spirit find little grace,
He was seal'd to Satan in any case,
Yet the loser had been the winner;
Had I waxed fainter or he less faint,
Then my soul was free from this loathsome taint,
I had died as a Christian knight—no saint
Perchance, yet a pardon'd sinner.

But I strove full grimly beneath his weight,

I clung to his poignard desperate,
I baffled the thrust that followed,
And writhing uppermost rose, to deal,
With bare three inches of broken steel,
One stroke—Ha! the headpiece crash'd piecemeal,
And the knave in his black blood wallow'd.

So I lived for worse—in fulness of time,
When peace for a season sway'd the clime,
And spears for a space were idle,
Trusted and chosen of all the court,
A favoured herald of fair report,
I travell'd eastward, and duly brought
A bride to a queenly bridal.

Pardie! 'twas a morning even as this
(The skies were warmer if aught, I wis,
Albeit the fields were duller;
Or it may be that the envious spring,
Abash'd at the sight of a fairer thing,
Wax'd somewhat sadder of colouring
Because of her faultless colour).

With her through the Lyonesse I rode,
Till the woods with the noontide fervour glow'd,
And there for a space we halted,
Where the intertwining branches made
Cool carpets of olive-tinted shade,
And the floors with fretwork of flame inlaid
From leafy lattices vaulted.

Adam Lindsay Gordon

And scarf and mantle for her I spread,
And strewed them over the grassiest bed,
And under the greenest awning,
And loosen'd latch and buckle, and freed
From selle and housing the red roan steed,
And the jennet of swift Iberian breed,
That had carried us since the dawning.

The brown thrush sang through the briar and bower,
All flush'd or frosted with forest flower
In the warm sun's wanton glances;
And I grew deaf to the song bird—blind
To blossom that sweeten'd the sweet spring wind—
I saw her only—a girl reclined
In her girlhood's indolent trances.

And the song and the scent and sense wax'd weak,
The wild rose withered beside the cheek
She poised on her fingers slender;
The soft spun gold of her glittering hair
Ran rippling into a wondrous snare,
That flooded the round arm bright and bare,
And the shoulder's silvery splendour.

The deep dusk fires in those dreamy eyes,
Like seas clear-coloured in summer skies,
Were guiltless of future treason;
And I stood watching her, still and mute,
Yet the evil seed in my soul found root,

And the sad plant throve, and the sinful fruit
Grew ripe in the shameful season.

Let the sin be mine as the shame was hers,
In desolate days of departed years
She had leisure for shame and sorrow—
There was light repentance and brief remorse,
When I rode against Saxon foes or Norse,
With clang of harness and clatter of horse,
And little heed for the morrow.

And now she is dead, men tell me, and I,
In this living death must I linger and lie
Till my cup to the dregs is drunken?
I looked through the lattice worn and grim,
With eyelids darken'd and eyesight dim,
And weary body and wasted limb,
And sinew slacken'd and shrunken.

She is dead! Gone down to the burial-place,
Where the grave-dews cleave to her faultless face;
Where the grave-sods crumble around her;
And that bright burden of burnish'd gold,
That once on those waxen shoulders roll'd,
Will it spoil with the damps of the deadly mould?
Was it shorn when the church vows bound her?

Now I know full well that the fair spear shaft
Shall never gladden my hand, nor the haft
Of the good sword grow to my fingers;

Adam Lindsay Gordon

Now the maddest fray, the merriest din,
Would fail to quicken this life-stream thin,
Yet the sleepy poison of that sweet sin
In the sluggish current still lingers.

Would God I had slept with the slain men, long
Or ever the heart conceived a wrong
That the innermost soul abhorred—
Or ever these lying lips were strained
To her lids, pearl-tinted and purple-vein'd,
Or ever those traitorous kisses stained
The snows of her spotless forehead.

Let me gather a little strength to think,
As one who reels on the outermost brink,
To the innermost gulf descending.
In that truce the longest and last of all,
In the summer nights of that festival—
Soft vesture of samite and silken pall—
The beginning came of the ending.

And one trod softly with sandal'd feet—
Ah! why are the stolen waters sweet?—
And one crept stealthily after;
I would I had taken him there and wrung
His knavish neck when the dark door swung,
Or torn by the roots his treacherous tongue,
And stifled his hateful laughter.

So the smouldering scandal blazed—but he,

My king, to the last put trust in me—
Aye, well was his trust requited!
Now priests may patter, and bells may toll,
He will need no masses to aid his soul;
When the angels open the judgment scroll,
His wrong will be tenfold righted.

Then dawn'd the day when the mail was donn'd,
And the steed for the strife caparison'd,
But not 'gainst the Norse invader.
Then was bloodshed—not by untoward chance,
As the blood that is drawn by the jouster's lance,
The fray in the castle of Melegrance,
The fight in the lists with Mador.

Then the guilt made manifest, then the siege,
When the true men rallying round the liege
Beleaguer'd his base betrayer;
Then the fruitless parleys, the pleadings vain,
And the hard-fought battles with brave Gawaine,
Twice worsted, and once so nearly slain,
I may well be counted his slayer.

Then the crime of Modred—a little sin
At the side of mine, though the knave was kin
To the king by the knave's hand stricken.
And the once-loved knight, was he there to save
That knightly king who that knighthood gave?
Ah, Christ! will he greet me as knight or knave
In the day when the dust shall quicken?

Adam Lindsay Gordon

Had he lightly loved, had he trusted less,
I had sinn'd perchance with the sinfulness
That through prayer and penance is pardoned.
Oh, love most loyal! Oh, faith most sure!
In the purity of a soul so pure
I found my safeguard—I sinn'd secure,
Till my heart to the sin grew harden'd.

We were glad together in gladsome meads,
When they shook to the strokes of our snorting steeds;
We were joyful in joyous lustre
When it flush'd the coppice or fill'd the glade,
Where the horn of the Dane or the Saxon bray'd,
And we saw the heathen banner display'd,
And the heathen lances cluster.

Then a steel-shod rush and a steel-clad ring,
And a crash of the spear staves splintering,
And the billowy battle blended.
Riot of chargers, revel of blows,
And fierce, flush'd faces of fighting foes,
From croup to bridle, that reel'd and rose,
In a sparkle of sword-play splendid.

And the long, lithe sword in the hand became
As a leaping light, as a falling flame,
As a fire through the flax that hasted;
Slender, and shining, and beautiful,
How it shore through shivering casque and skull,

And never a stroke was void and null,
And never a thrust was wasted.

I have done for ever with all these things—
Deeds that were joyous to knights and kings,
In days that with songs were cherish'd.
The songs are ended, the deeds are done,
There shall none of them gladden me now, not one;
There is nothing good for me under the sun,
But to perish as these things perish'd.

Shall it profit me aught that the bishop seeks
My presence daily, and duly speaks
Soft words of comfort and kindness?
Shall it aught avail me? "Certes," he said,
"Though thy soul is darken'd, be not afraid—
God hateth nothing that He hath made—
His light shall disperse thy blindness."

I am not afraid for myself, although
I know I have had that light, and I know
The greater my condemnation.
When I well-nigh swoon'd in the deep-drawn bliss
Of that first long, sweet, slow, stolen kiss,
I would gladly have given, for less than this,
Myself, with my soul's salvation.

I would languish thus in some loathsome den,
As a thing of naught in the eyes of men,
In the mouths of men as a by-word,

Adam Lindsay Gordon

Through years of pain, and when God saw fit,
Singing his praises my soul should flit
To the darkest depth of the nethermost pit,
If *hers* could be wafted skyward.

Lord Christ! have patience a little while,
I have sinn'd because I am utterly vile,
Having light, loving darkness rather.
And I pray Thee deal with me as Thou wilt,
Yet the blood of Thy foes I have freely spilt,
And, moreover, mine is the greater guilt
In the sight of Thee and Thy Father.

That saint, Thy servant, was counted dear
Whose sword in the garden grazed the ear
Of Thine enemy, Lord Redeemer!
Not thus on the shattering visor jarr'd
In this hand the iron of the hilt cross-barr'd,
When the blade was swallow'd up to the guard
Through the teeth of the strong blasphemer.

If ever I smote as a man should smite,
If I struck one stroke that seem'd good in Thy sight,
By Thy loving mercy prevailing,
Lord! Let her stand in the light of Thy face,
Cloth'd with Thy love and crown'd with Thy grace,
When I gnash my teeth in the terrible place
That is fill'd with weeping and wailing.

Shall I comfort my soul on account of this?

In the world to come, whatsoever it is,
There is no more earthly ill-doing—
For the dusty darkness shall slay desire,
And the chaff may burn with unquenchable fire,
But for green wild growth of thistle and briar
At least there is no renewing.

And this grievous burden of life shall change
In the dim hereafter, dreamy and strange,
And sorrows and joys diurnal.
And partial blessings and perishing ills
Shall fade in the praise, or the pang that fills
The glory of God's eternal hills,
Or the gloom of His gulf eternal.

Yet if all things change to the glory of One
Who for all ill-doers gave His Own sweet Son,
To His goodness so shall He change ill,
When the world as a wither'd leaf shall be,
And the sky like a shrivell'd scroll shall flee,
And souls shall be summon'd from land and sea,
At the blast of His bright archangel.

"Cadger"
Pen and ink sketch by Adam Lindsay Gordon
State Library of Victoria, ID3455661.

Thora's Song

[From *Astaroth: A Dramatic Lyric*]

We severed in autumn early,
Ere the earth was torn by the plough;
The wheat and the oats and the barley
Are ripe for the harvest now.
We sunder'd one misty morning,
Ere the hills were dimm'd by the rain,
Through the flowers those hills adorning—
Thou comest not back again.

My heart is heavy and weary
With the weight of a weary soul;
The mid-day glare grows dreary,
And dreary the midnight scroll.
The corn-stalks sigh for the sickle,
'Neath the load of the golden grain;
I sigh for a mate more fickle—
Thou comest not back again.

The warm sun riseth and setteth,
The night bringeth moist'ning dew,
But the soul that longeth forgetteth
The warmth and the moisture, too;
In the hot sun rising and setting
There is naught save feverish pain;
There are tears in the night-dews wetting—
Thou comest not back again.

Adam Lindsay Gordon

Thy voice in mine ear still mingles
With the voices of whisp'ring trees;
Thy kiss on my cheek still tingles
At each kiss of the summer breeze;
While dreams of the past are thronging
For substance of shades in vain,
I am waiting, watching, and longing—
Thou comest not back again.

Waiting and watching ever,
Longing and lingering yet,
Leaves rustle and corn-stalks quiver,
Winds murmur and waters fret;
No answer they bring, no greeting,
No speech save that sad refrain,
No voice, save an echo repeating—
He cometh not back again.

The Three Friends

[From the French]

The sword slew one in deadly strife;
One perish'd by the bowl;
The third lies self-slain by the knife;
For three the bells may toll—
I loved her better than my life,
And better than my soul.

Aye, father! Hast thou come at last?
'Tis somewhat late to pray;
Life's crimson tides are ebbing fast,
They drain my soul away;
Mine eyes with film are overcast,
The lights are waning grey.

This curl from her bright head I shore,
And this her hands gave mine;
See, one is stained with purple gore,
And one with poison'd wine;
Give these to her when all is o'er—
How serpent-like they twine!

We three were brethren in arms,
And sworn companions we;
We held this motto, "Whoso harms
The one shall harm the three!"
Till, matchless for her subtle charms,

Adam Lindsay Gordon

Beloved of each was she.

(These two were slain that I might kiss
Her sweet mouth. I did well;
I said, "There is no greater bliss
For those in heaven that dwell;"
I lost her; then I said, "There is
No fiercer pang in hell!")

We have upheld each other's rights,
Shared purse, and borrow'd blade;
Have stricken side by side in fights;
And side by side have prayed
In churches. We were Christian knights,
And she a Christian maid.

We met at sunrise, he and I,
My comrade—'twas agreed
The steel our quarrel first should try,
The poison should succeed;
For two of three were doom'd to die,
And one was doomed to bleed.

We buckled to the doubtful fray,
At first with some remorse;
But he who must be slain, or slay,
Soon strikes with vengeful force.
He fell; I left him where he lay,
Among the trampled gorse.

Did passion warp my heart and head
To madness? And, if so,
Can madness palliate bloodshed?—
It may be—I shall know
When God shall gather up the dead
From where the four winds blow.

We met at sunset, he and I—
My second comrade true;
Two cups with wine were brimming high,
And one was drugg'd—we knew
Not which, nor sought we to descry;
Our choice by lot we drew.

And there I sat with him to sup;
I heard him blithely speak
Of by-gone days—the fatal cup
Forgotten seem'd—his cheek
Was ruddy: father, raise me up,
My voice is waxing weak.

We drank; his lips turned livid white,
His cheeks grew leaden ash;
He reel'd—I heard his temples smite
The threshold with a crash!
And from his hand, in shivers bright,
I saw the goblet flash.

The morrow dawn'd with fragrance rare,
The May breeze, from the west,

Adam Lindsay Gordon

Just fann'd the sleepy olives, where
She heard and I confess'd;
My hair entangled with her hair,
Her breast strained to my breast.

On the dread verge of endless gloom
My soul recalls that hour;
Skies languishing with balm of bloom,
And fields aflame with flower;
And slow caresses that consume,
And kisses that devour.

Ah! Now with storm the day seems rife,
My dull ears catch the roll
Of thunder, and the far sea strife,
On beach and bar and shoal—
I loved her better than my life,
And better than my soul.

She fled! I cannot prove her guilt,
Nor would I an I could;
See, life for life is fairly spilt!
And blood is shed for blood;
Her white hands neither touched the hilt,
Nor yet the potion brew'd.

Aye! Turn me from the sickly south,
Towards the gusty north;
The fruits of sin are dust and drouth,
The end of crime is wrath—

The lips that pressed her rose-like mouth
Are choked with blood-red froth.

Then dig the grave-pit deep and wide,
Three graves thrown into one,
And lay three corpses side by side,
And tell their tale to none;
But bring her back in all her pride
To see what she hath done.

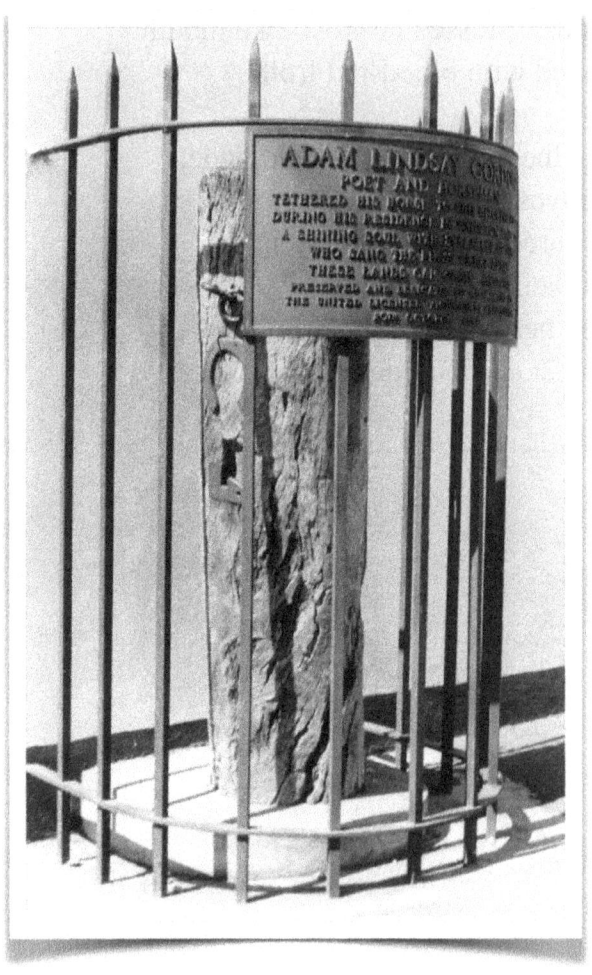

The hitching post used by Adam Lindsay Gordon at the Marine Hotel, Brighton, VIC. © State Library of Victoria, ID1670179. Used in line with SLV permissions.

A Song of Autumn

"Where shall we go for our garlands glad
At the falling of the year,
When the burnt-up banks are yellow and sad,
When the boughs are yellow and sere?
Where are the old ones that once we had,
And when are the new ones near?
What shall we do for our garlands glad
At the falling of the year?"

"Child! can I tell where the garlands go?
Can I say where the lost leaves veer
On the brown-burnt banks, when the wild winds blow,
When they drift through the dead-wood drear?
Girl! When the garlands of next year glow,
You may gather again, my dear—
But I go where the last year's lost leaves go
At the falling of the year."

Adam Lindsay Gordon

The Romance of Britomarte

As related by Sergeant Leigh on the night he got his
captaincy at the Restoration.

I'll tell you a story; but pass the "jack",
And let us make merry to-night, my men.
Aye, those were the days when my beard was black—
I like to remember them now and then—
Then Miles was living, and Cuthbert there,
On his lip was never a sign of down;
But I carry about some braided hair,
That has not yet changed from the glossy brown
That it showed the day when I broke the heart
Of that bravest of destriers, "Britomarte".

Sir Hugh was slain (may his soul find grace!)
In the fray that was neither lost nor won
At Edgehill—then to St. Hubert's Chase
Lord Goring despatched a garrison—
But men and horses were ill to spare,
And ere long the soldiers were shifted fast.
As for me, I never was quartered there
Till Marston Moor had been lost; at last,
As luck would have it, alone, and late
In the night, I rode to the northern gate.

I thought, as I passed through the moonlit park,
On the boyish days I used to spend
In the halls of the knight lying stiff and stark—

Thought on his lady, my father's friend
(Mine, too, in spite of my sinister bar,
But with that my story has naught to do)—
She died the winter before the war;
Died giving birth to the baby Hugh.
He pass'd ere the green leaves clothed the bough,
And the orphan girl was the heiress now.

When I was a rude and a reckless boy,
And she a brave and a beautiful child,
I was her page, her playmate, her toy—
I have crown'd her hair with the field-flowers wild,
Cowslip and crowfoot and coltsfoot bright—
I have carried her miles when the woods were wet,
I have read her romances of dame and knight;
She was my princess, my pride, my pet,
There was then this proverb us twain between,
For the glory of God and of Gwendoline.

She had grown to a maiden wonderful fair,
But for years I had scarcely seen her face.
Now, with troopers Holdsworth, Huntly, and Clare,
Old Miles kept guard at St. Hubert's Chase,
And the chatelaine was a Mistress Ruth,
Sir Hugh's half-sister, an ancient dame,
But a mettlesome soul had she forsooth,
As she show'd when the time of her trial came.
I bore despatches to Miles and to her,
To warn them against the bands of Kerr.

Adam Lindsay Gordon

And mine would have been a perilous ride
With the rebel horsemen—we knew not where
They were scattered over that country side,—
If it had not been for my brave brown mare.
She was iron-sinew'd and satin-skinn'd,
Ribb'd like a drum and limb'd like a deer,
Fierce as the fire and fleet as the wind—
There was nothing she couldn't climb or clear—
Rich lords had vex'd me, in vain, to part,
For their gold and silver, with Britomarte.

Next morn we muster'd scarce half a score,
With the serving men, who were poorly arm'd—
Five soldiers, counting myself, no more,
And a culverin, which might well have harm'd
Us, had we used it, but not our foes,
When, with horses and foot, to our doors they came,
And a psalm-singer summon'd us (through his nose),
And deliver'd—"This, in the people's name,
Unto whoso holdeth this fortress here,
Surrender! Or bide the siege—John Kerr."

'Twas a mansion built in a style too new,
A castle by courtesy, he lied
Who called it a fortress—yet, 'tis true,
It had been indifferently fortified—
We were well provided with bolt and bar—
And while I hurried to place our men,
Old Miles was call'd to a council of war
With Mistress Ruth and with *her*, and when

They had argued loudly and long, those three,
They sent, as a last resource, for me.

In the chair of state sat erect Dame Ruth;
She had cast aside her embroidery;
She had been a beauty, they say, in her youth,
There was much fierce fire in her bold black eye.
"Am I deceived in you both?" quoth she.
"If one spark of her father's spirit lives
In this girl here—so, this Leigh, Ralph Leigh,
Let us hear what counsel the springald gives."
Then I stammer'd, somewhat taken aback—
(Simon, you ale-swiller, pass the "jack").

The dame wax'd hotter—"Speak out, lad, say,
Must we fall in that canting caitiff's power?
Shall we yield to a knave and a turncoat? Nay,
I had liever leap from our topmost tower.
For a while we can surely await relief;
Our walls are high and our doors are strong."
This Kerr was indeed a canting thief—
I know not rightly, some private wrong
He had done Sir Hugh, but I know this much,
Traitor or turncoat, he suffer'd as such.

Quoth Miles—"Enough! your will shall be done;
Relief may arrive by the merest chance,
But your house ere dusk will be lost and won;
They have got three pieces of ordnance."
Then I cried, "Lord Guy, with four troops of horse,

Adam Lindsay Gordon

Even now is biding at Westbrooke town;
If a rider could break through the rebel force,
He would bring relief ere the sun goes down;
Through the postern door could I make one dart,
I could baffle them all upon Britomarte."

Miles mutter'd "Madness!" Dame Ruth look'd grave,
Said, "True, though we cannot keep one hour
The courtyard, no, nor the stables save,
They will have to batter piecemeal the tower,
And thus——" But suddenly she halted there.
With a shining hand on my shoulder laid
Stood Gwendoline. She had left her chair,
And, "Nay, if it needs must be done," she said,
"Ralph Leigh will gladly do it, I ween,
For the glory of God and of Gwendoline."

I had undertaken a heavier task
For a lighter word. I saddled with care,
Nor cumber'd myself with corselet nor casque
(Being loth to burden the brave brown mare).
Young Clare kept watch on the wall—he cried,
"Now, haste, Ralph! this is the time to seize;
The rebels are round us on every side,
But here they straggle by twos and threes."
Then out I led her, and up I sprung,
And the postern door on its hinges swung.

I had drawn this sword—you may draw it and feel,
For this is the blade that I bore that day—

There's a notch even now on the long grey steel,
A nick that has never been rasp'd away.
I bow'd my head and I buried my spurs,
One bound brought the gliding green beneath;
I could tell by her back-flung, flatten'd ears,
She had fairly taken the bit in her teeth—
(What, Jack, have you drain'd your namesake dry,
Left nothing to quench the thirst of a fly?)

These things are done, and are done with, lad,
In far less time than your talker tells;
The sward with their hoof-strokes shook like mad,
And rang with their carbines and petronels;
And they shouted, "Cross him and cut him off,"
"Surround him," "Seize him," "Capture the clown,
Or kill him," "Shall he escape to scoff
In your faces?" "Shoot him or cut him down."
And their bullets whistled on every side;
Many were near us and more were wide.

Not a bullet told upon Britomarte;
Suddenly snorting, she launched along;
So the osprey dives where the seagulls dart,
So the falcon swoops where the kestrels throng.
And full in my front one pistol flash'd,
And right in my path their sergeant got.
How are jack-boots jarr'd, how are stirrups clash'd,
While the mare like a meteor past him shot;
But I clove his skull with a backstroke clean,
For the glory of God and of Gwendoline.

Adam Lindsay Gordon

And as one whom the fierce wind storms in the face,
With spikes of hail and with splinters of rain,
I, while we fled through St. Hubert's Chase,
Bent till my cheek was amongst her mane.
To the north, full a league of the deer-park lay,
Smooth, springy turf, and she fairly flew,
And the sound of their hoof-strokes died away,
And their far shots faint in the distance grew.
Loudly I laughed, having won the start,
At the folly of following Britomarte.

They had posted a guard at the northern gate—
Some dozen of pikemen and musketeers.
To the tall park palings I turn'd her straight;
She veer'd in her flight as the swallow veers.
And some blew matches and some drew swords,
And one of them wildly hurl'd his pike,
But she clear'd by inches the oaken boards,
And she carried me yards beyond the dyke;
Then gaily over the long green down
We gallop'd, heading for Westbrooke town.

The green down slopes to the great grey moor,
The grey moor sinks to the gleaming Skelt—
Sudden and sullen, and swift and sure,
The whirling water was round my belt.
She breasted the bank with a savage snort,
And a backward glance of her bloodshot eye,
And "Our Lady of Andover's" flash'd like thought,

And flitted St. Agatha's nunnery,
And the firs at "The Ferngrove" fled on the right,
And "Falconer's Tower" on the left took flight.

And over "The Ravenswold" we raced—
We rounded the hill by "The Hermit's Well"—
We burst on the Westbrooke Bridge—"What haste?
What errand?" shouted the sentinel.
"To Beelzebub with the Brewer's knave!"
"*Carolus Rex* and he of the Rhine!"
Galloping past him, I got and gave
In the gallop password and countersign,
All soak'd with water and soil'd with mud,
With the sleeve of my jerkin half drench'd in blood.

Now, Heaven be praised that I found him there—
Lord Guy. He said, having heard my tale,
"Leigh, let my own man look to your mare,
Rest and recruit with our wine and ale;
But first must our surgeon attend to you;
You are somewhat shrewdly stricken, no doubt."
Then he snatched a horn from the wall and blew,
Making "Boot and Saddle" ring sharply out.
"Have I done good service this day?" quoth I.
"Then I will ride back in your troop, Lord Guy."

In the street I heard how the trumpets peal'd,
And I caught the gleam of a morion
From the window—then to the door I reel'd;
I had lost more blood than I reckon'd upon;

Adam Lindsay Gordon

He eyed me calmly with keen grey eyes—
Stern grey eyes of a steel-blue grey—
Said, "The wilful man can never be wise,
Nathless, the wilful must have his way,"
And he pour'd from a flagon some fiery wine;
I drain'd it, and straightway strength was mine.

I was with them all the way on the brown—
"Guy to the rescue!" "God and the king!"
We were just in time, for the doors were down;
And didn't our sword-blades rasp and ring,
And didn't we hew and didn't we hack?
The sport scarce lasted minutes ten—
(Aye, those were the days when my beard was black;
I like to remember them now and then).
Though they fought like fiends, we were four to one,
And we captured those that refused to run.

We have not forgotten it, Cuthbert, boy!
That supper scene when the lamps were lit;
How the women (some of them) sobb'd for joy,
How the soldiers drank the deeper for it;
How the dame did honours, and Gwendoline,
How grandly she glided into the hall,
How she stoop'd with the grace of a girlish queen,
And kiss'd me gravely before them all;
And the stern Lord Guy, how gaily he laugh'd,
Till more of his cup was spilt than quaff'd.

Brown Britomarte lay dead in her straw

Next morn—we buried her—brave old girl!
John Kerr, we tried him by martial law,
And we twisted some hemp for the trait'rous churl;
And she—I met her alone—said she,
"You have risk'd your life, you have lost your mare,
And what can I give in return, Ralph Leigh?"
I replied, "One braid of that bright brown hair."
And with that she bow'd her beautiful head,
"You can take as much as you choose," she said.

And I took it—it may be, more than enough—
And I shore it rudely, close to the roots.
The wine or wounds may have made me rough,
And men at the bottom are merely brutes.
Three weeks I slept at St. Hubert's Chase;
When I woke from the fever of wounds and wine,
I could scarce believe that the ghastly face
That the glass reflected was really mine.
I sought the hall—where a wedding *had been*—
The wedding of Guy and of Gwendoline.

The romance of a grizzled old trooper's life
May make you laugh in your sleeves: laugh out,
Lads; we have most of us seen some strife;
We have all of us had some sport, no doubt.
I have won some honour and gain'd some gold,
Now that our king returns to his own;
If the pulses beat slow, if the blood runs cold,
And if friends have faded and loves have flown,
Then the greater reason is ours to drink,

Adam Lindsay Gordon

And the more we swallow the less we shall think.

At the battle of Naseby, Miles was slain,
And Huntly sank from his wounds that week;
We left young Clare upon Worcester plain—
How the "Ironside" gash'd his girlish cheek.
Aye, strut, and swagger, and ruffle anew,
Gay gallants, now that the war is done!
They fought like fiends (give the fiend his due)—
We fought like fops, it was thus they won.
Holdsworth is living for aught I know,
At least he was living two years ago,

And Guy—Lord Guy—so stately and stern,
He is changed, I met him at Winchester;
He has grown quite gloomy and taciturn.
Gwendoline!—why do you ask for her?
Died as her mother had died before—
Died giving birth to the baby Guy!
Did my voice shake? Then am I fool the more.
Sooner or later we all must die;
But, at least, let us live while we live to-night.
The *days* may be dark, but the *lamps* are bright.

For to me the sunlight seems worn and wan:
The sun, he is losing his splendour now—
He can never shine as of old he shone
On her glorious hair and glittering brow.
Ah! those *days that were*, when my beard was black,
Now I have only the *nights that are*.

What, landlord, ho! Bring in haste burnt sack,
And a flask of your fiercest usquebaugh.
You, Cuthbert! surely you know by heart
The story of *her* and of Britomarte.

Flemington Racecourse, 1867
Adam Lindsay Gordon is said to be
one of the riders pictured.
Painting by T. H. Lyttleton
State Library of Victoria, ID1678496.

Laudamus

The Lord shall slay or the Lord shall save!
He is righteous whether He save or slay—
Brother, give thanks for the gifts He gave,
Though the gifts He gave He hath taken away.
Shall we strive for that which is nothing? Nay.
Shall we hate each other for that which fled?
She is but a marvel of modelled clay,
And the smooth, clear white, and the soft, pure red,
That we coveted, shall endure no day.

Was it wise or well that I hated you
For the fruit that hung too high on the tree?
For the blossom out of our reach that grew,
Was it well or wise that you hated me?—
My hate has flown, and your hate shall flee.
Let us veil our faces like children chid—
Can that violet orb we swore by see
Through that violet-vein'd, transparent lid?—
Now the Lord forbid that this strife should be.

Would you knit the forehead or clench the fist,
For the curls that never were well caress'd—
For the red that never was fairly kiss'd—
For the white that never was fondly press'd?
Shall we nourish wrath while she lies at rest
Between us? Surely our wrath shall cease.
We would fain know better—the Lord knows best—
Is there peace between us? Yea, there is peace,

Adam Lindsay Gordon

In the soul's release she at least is blest.

Let us thank the Lord for His bounties all,
For the brave old days of pleasure and pain,
When the world for both of us seem'd too small—
Though the love was void and the hate was vain—
Though the word was bitter between us twain,
And the bitter word was kin to the blow,
For her gloss and ripple of rich gold rain,
For her velvet crimson and satin snow—
Though we never shall know the old days again.

The Lord!—His mercy is great, men say;
His wrath, men say, is a burning brand—
Let us praise Him whether He save or slay,
And above her body let hand join hand.
We shall meet, my friend, in the spirit land—
Will our strife renew? Nay, I dare not trust,
For the grim, great gulf that cannot be spann'd
Will divide us from her. The Lord is just,
She shall not be thrust where our spirits stand.

A Basket of Flowers

[From Dawn to Dusk]

Dawn

On skies still and starlit
White lustres take hold,
And grey flushes scarlet,
And red flashes gold.
And sun-glories cover
The rose shed above her,
Like lover and lover
They flame and unfold.

* * * * *

Still bloom in the garden
Green grass-plot, fresh lawn,
Though pasture lands harden
And drought fissures yawn.
While leaves not a few fall,
Let rose leaves for you fall,
Leaves pearl-strung with dew-fall,
And gold shot with dawn.

Does the grass-plot remember
The fall of your feet
In Autumn's red ember,

When drought leagues with heat,
When the last of the roses
Despairingly closes
In the lull that reposes
Ere storm winds wax fleet?

Love's melodies languish
In "Chastelard's" strain,
And "Abelard's" anguish
Is love's pleasant pain;
And "Sappho" rehearses
Love's blessings and curses
In passionate verses
Again and again.

And I!—I have heard of
All these long ago,
Yet never one word of
Their song-lore I know;
Not under my finger
In songs of the singer
Love's litanies linger,
Love's rhapsodies flow.

Fresh flowers in a basket—
An offering to you—
Though you did not ask it,
Unbidden I strew;
With heat and drought striving,
Some blossoms still living

May render thanksgiving
For dawn and for dew.

The garlands I gather,
The rhymes I string fast,
Are hurriedly rather
Than heedlessly cast.
Yon tree's shady awning
Is short'ning, and warning
Far spent is the morning,
And I must ride fast.

Songs empty, yet airy,
I've striven to write,
For failure, dear Mary!
Forgive me—Good-night!
Songs and flowers may beset you,
I can only regret you,
While the soil where I met you
Recedes from my sight.

For the sake of past hours,
For the love of old times,
Take "A Basket of Flowers",
And a bundle of rhymes;
Though all the bloom perish
E'en *your* hand can cherish,
While churlish and bearish
The verse-jingle chimes.

Adam Lindsay Gordon

And Eastward by Nor'ward
Looms sadly *my* track,
And I must ride forward,
And still I look back,—
Look back—ah, how vainly!
For while I see plainly,
My hands on the reins lie
Uncertain and slack.

The warm wind breathes strong breath,
The dust dims mine eye,
And I draw one long breath,
And stifle one sigh.
Green slopes, softly shaded,
Have flitted and faded—
My dreams flit as they did—
Good-night!—and—Good-bye!

* * * * *

Dusk

Last rose! End my story!
Dead core and dry husk—
Departed thy glory
And tainted thy musk.
Night spreads her dark limbs on
The face of the dim sun,
So flame fades to crimson
And crimson to dusk.

A Fragment

They say that poison-sprinkled flowers
Are sweeter in perfume
Than when, untouched by deadly dew,
They glowed in early bloom.

They say that men condemned to die
Have quaffed the sweetened wine
With higher relish than the juice
Of the untampered vine.

They say that in the witch's song,
Though rude and harsh it be,
There blends a wild, mysterious strain
Of weirdest melody.

And I believe the devil's voice
Sinks deeper in our ear
Than any whisper sent from Heaven,
However sweet and clear.

Adam Lindsay Gordon

Bust of Australian poet Adam Lindsay Gordon. Poets' Corner in Westminster Abbey. Unveiled in 1934. Sculpted by Kathleen Scott. Photo by 14GTR, 26 July 2022. CC-BY-SA 4.0

Adam Lindsay Gordon

Review: The Argus (Melbourne)

Tuesday, 28th June, 1870

BUSH BALLADS AND GALLOPING RHYMES

These poems were placed in our hands for review three days before the melancholy fate of their author became the "sensational topic" of an hour for the world, who best knew him as the daring steeplechase rider and eccentric man of talent, and the subject of earnest and wondering sorrow among those intimate friends who admired him for his warm heart and his generous sympathies no less than for his reckless courage and his rare abilities.

Mr. Gordon was a man of cultivated and refined mind, and of more than average literary taste and talent. It is more than probable that, had he lived a few years longer, he would have made for himself a reputation of no ordinary character. His ballads, "Bush Ballads," as he called them —were spirited and rhythmical, instinct with the genius of the scenes that inspired them. Although he affected Swinburne and Browning, and drew considerably upon the storehouse of epithet and adjective which those gentlemen have left unlocked for the use of future generations, he displayed a natural vigour and force which trended upon, if it did not touch, originality. Neat in translation, and with an intuitive knowledge and appreciation of the spirit of his author, Mr. Gordon's few renderings of French and

German poems are made with boldness and ease. One feels that the same dominant idea which prompted the original has been divined and expressed in the translation, and that the verses are not mere dull transcriptions of translated words, but rather happy transplantations of thoughts from one language to another. As an example of this we may quote the "Three Friends," a passionate lyric in which the spirit and soul of the original gleams in every line, though perhaps not one single verse could be "put back" into the French which inspired it. But where Mr. Gordon was most at home was in those rollicking, daredevil ballads which are born of the jingle of bridle and the clatter of hoofs. The cavalier songs of the Restoration have inspired many a balladmaker since Scott, Aytoun, and Macaulay, but, if we except Mr. Walter Thornbury's "Boot and Saddle,"

"Stirrup well hung,
Carabine slung,
Flask at the saddlebow merrily swung;
Troopers advance! By the lillies of France
We are the gallants to lead them a dance!",

we have read nothing like Mr. Gordon's "Britomarte," since Young Lochinvar bore his bride over the border.

A fearless rider and a thorough sportsman, the author of "Bush Ballads" drew much of his inspiration from the excitement of the field, and his "Galloping Rhymes" are free and bounding as the stride of a good horse. For instance, "How we beat the favourite":

"The fourth fence, a wattle, floor'd Monk and Bluebottle;
The Drag came to grief at the blackthorn and ditch;
The rails toppled over Redoubt and Red Rover,
The lane stopped Lycurgus and Leicestershire Witch.
She passed like an arrow Kildara and Cock Sparrow,
And Mantrap and Mermaid refused the stone wall;
And Giles on The Greyling came down at the paling,
And I was left sailing in front of them all."

The metre of those two stanzas may vie in effect with the too celebrated dactyllic line in Virgil; while,

"She raced at the rasper, I felt my knees grasp her,
I found my hands give to her strain on the bit,
She rose when The Clown did—our silks as we bounded
Brush'd lightly; our stirrups clash'd loud as we lit"

displays a knowledge of horsemanship and an experience of the saddle which was not vouchsafed to the somewhat prosy bard of Mantua.

But Mr. Gordon's faults were as perceptible as his beauties. His style was careless to ungainliness, and he seems to have written as he rode, with his eyes on the last fence, and never a look to right or left. Such rhymes as "best word" and "restward," "Achilles" and "lillies," "we are ill" and "evil," "perdus" and "their due," "green leaf" and "e'en lief," mar some of his best verses; while haste of composition can alone excuse such lines as,

"The sward with their hoof strokes rang like mad."

or,

"Flash! flash! bang! bang! and we blazed away
And the grey roof reddened and rang
Flash! flash! and I felt his bullet flay
The tip of my ear. Flash! bang!",

while such expressions as "the fragrance of bearish roses," and the "music of parched-up rills" are simply nonsense. The dedication—to Captain Whyte Melville—is strained in sentiment and affected in diction, and is moreover, in intention and phraseology, plagiarised from Swinburne:—

"They are rhymes rudely strung, with intent less of
    sound than of words,
In lands were bright blossoms are scentless, and
    songless bright birds.
Where the fire and fierce drought on her tresses,
Insatiable summer oppresses
Sere woodlands, and sad wildernesses,
And faint flocks and herds."

Adam Lindsay Gordon

Apart from the false quantity in the last line but one – "wilderness" is a word of four short syllables – an error which Swinburne would not have committed, and an attempt to disguise the rhythm by the insertion of an extra rhyming line, the influence of the dedication of "Poems and Ballads" is very apparent. The "De Te," a very sad and terrible poem, owes something, especially in the quaintness of the eighth verse, to Browning, and all with its strong interest and grave suggestiveness is likely on that account to be passed without comment.

But when Mr. Gordon stood on his own ground, and drew solely upon his own powers, he could write stirringly and well. The ballad of "Britomarte" is among the best things in the volume. It is the story of a soldier of fortune, who is a trooper in a Royalist regiment. When a boy he was brought up with the baby heiress of the Royalist Sir Hugh, and learns to love her.

> "When I was a rude and a reckless boy,
> And she a brave and a beautiful child,
> I was her page, her playmate, her toy—
> I have crown'd her hair with the field-flowers wild,
> Cowslip and crowfoot, and coltsfoot bright—
> I have carried her miles when the woods were wet,
> I have read her romances of dame and knight—
> She was my princess, my pride, my pet.
> There was then this proverb us twain between,
> For the glory of God and of Gwendoline."

The Roundheads attack the castle. Lord Guy with four troops of horse is at Westbrook Town. A bold rider on a staunch horse might run the gauntlet of the guard and Leigh volunteers to risk his own life and that of his brown mare for the memory of his password:

"These things are done, and are done with, lad,
In far less time than your talker tells.
The sward with their hoof strokes shook like mad,
And rang with their carbines and petronels,
And they shouted, 'Cross him and cut him off,'
'Surround him,' 'Seize him,' 'Capture the clown
Or kill him,' 'Shall he escape to scoff
In your faces ?' 'Shoot him or cut him down.'
And their bullets whistled on every side:
Many were near us and more were wide.

"Not a bullet told upon Britomarte—
Suddenly snorting, she launched along—
So the osprey dives where the seagulls dart,
So the falcon swoops whore the kestrels throng ;
And full in my front one pistol flash'd,
And right in my path their sergeant got.
How our jack-boots jarr'd, how our stirrups clash'd,
While the mare like a meteor past him shot ;
But I clove his skull with a backstroke clean,
For the glory of God and of Gwendoline."

He escapes, leaps the fence, gallops over the moor, and brings the rescue. His heroine is saved, and marries Lord

Adam Lindsay Gordon

Guy. Sergeant Leigh tells the story of his brave brown mare over a jack of ale, and laughs because he feels the tears in his throat.

> "Did my voice shake? Then am I fool the more.
> Sooner or later we all must die:
> But at least, let us live while we live to-night.
> The days may be dark, but the lamps are bright,
> For to me the sunlight seems worn and wan:
> The sun, he is losing his splendour now -
> He never can shine as of old he shone
> On her glorious hair and glittering brow.
> Ah ! those days that were, when my beard was black;
> Now I have only the nights that are.
> What, landlord, ho! bring in haste burnt sack
> And a flask of your fiercest usquebagh.
> You, Cuthbert! surely you know by heart
> The story of her and of Britomarte."

A somewhat lengthy ballad, called "The Ride from the Wreck," is descriptive and dramatic. "Laudamus" is powerful; and "No Name"—the story of a seduced woman—has something of that savage intensity of passion which belongs to the German; but, next to "De Te," the most complete poem in the book, we place "The Sick Stockrider." Indeed, this simple and touching story is written with so true an eye for colour, and so happy a sympathy with human feeling, that it will be more admired than the gloomy speculation and ill-boding horror of the first mentioned poem. The sick man is riding painfully into the home station with his friend, when a faintness overcomes him. He sees the familiar mountains, the well-known roofs, the oft-gazed at beauties of plain and river, and his memory goes back to the "old days" and of his rough pulseful life.

> "In these hours when life is ebbing, how those days when life was young
> Come back to us—how clearly I recall
> Even the yarns Jack Hall invented, and the songs Jem Roper sung.
> And where are now Jem Roper and Jack Hall?
> Ay! nearly all our comrades of the old colonial school,
> Our ancient boon companions, Ned, are gone;
> Hard livers for the most part, somewhat reckless as a rule,
> It seems that you and I are left alone.
>
> "There was Hughes, who got in trouble through that business with the cards,
> It matters little what became of him.
> But a steer ripp'd up Macpherson in the Cooraminta yards,
> And Sullivan was drown'd at Sink-or-Swim,
> And Mostyn—poor Frank Mostyn—died at last a fearful wreck,
> In 'the horrors' at the Upper Wandinong,
> And Carisbrooke the rider at the Horsefall broke his neck,

Adam Lindsay Gordon

Faith! the wonder was he saved his neck so long!
Ah ! those days and nights we squandered at the Logans
   in the Glen—
The Logans, man and wife, have long been dead,
Elsie's tallest girl seems taller than your little Elsie
   then,
And Ethel is a woman grown and wed.

I've had my share of pastime, and I've done my share
   of toil,
And life is short—the longest life a span—
I care not now to tarry for the corn or for the oil,
Or for the wine that maketh glad the heart of man;
For good undone and gifts misspent and resolutions
   vain,
'Tis somewhat late to trouble—This I know,
I should live the same life over, if I had to live again;
And the chances are I go where most men go.

The deep blue skies wax dusky, and the tall green trees
   grow dim,
The sward beneath me seems to heave and fall,
And sickly, smoky shadows through the sleepy sunlight
   swim.
And on the very sun's face weave their pall.
Let me slumber in the hollow where the wattle
   blossoms wave,
With never stone or rail to fence my bed;
Should the sturdy station children pull the bush flowers
   on my grave,

I may chance to hear them romping overhead."

The strain of complaint and pain, which, when not pushed into reckless gaiety, or forgotten in the momentary excitement of furious gallop of horse and verse, seems to us to run through all that Mr. Gordon has written, is less here apparent, and with it we prefer to close our notice of the volume.

He has done nothing great, but has shown capacity for much, and his very shortcomings made us the more eager to see him attain the goal he was better qualified to reach than most. His acute sensibility, reckless carelessness of life, and a strong poetic temperament, operating through a physically injured brain, was perhaps the cause of his melancholy fate. As he himself wrote not many weeks before his end:

> "Aye what they will, such trifles kill.
> Comrade, for one good deed of yours,
> Your history shall not help to fill
> The mouths of many brainless boors.
> It may be death absolves or cures
> The sin of life. 'Twere hazardous
> To assert so. If the sin endures,
> Say only. 'God who has judged him thus,
> Be merciful to him, and us.'"

Adam Lindsay Gordon

Bush Ballads

Thanks for reading!

The audiobook version of *Bush Ballads and Galloping Rhymes* by Adam Lindsay Gordon, narrated by Roger Parish, is available at all good audiobook retailers.

For more information about Voices of Today, or to view our catalogue, please visit
www.voicesoftoday.org

Bush Ballads

www.ingramcontent.com/pod-product-compliance
Lightning Source LLC
Chambersburg PA
CBHW060156050426
42446CB00013B/2854